Active Auditing

A Practical Guide to Lean & Agile Auditing

by Prescott Coleman, CIA, CISA, MBA

Edited by
Sandy Kasahara, CPA, CIA
Version 1.1

ISBN: 9781092839303
Imprint: Independently published

DEDICATED TO

All the auditors and clients who put up with me before I figured all this
out.

CONTENTS

ACKNOWLEDGMENTS

In the writing of this book, I wish to thank...

My wife, Elizabeth, who never once questioned that I was writing a book and just assumed it would be worthwhile.

My editor, Sandy, who was the first to express that there was something here worth saying.

Jennifer, Scott, and Cheryl, who helped build Active Auditing with their wisdom, effort, courage, and willingness to experiment.

The board, management and staff (particularly Angela, Stephanie, Paula, and Jeff) of Denver Water, who were willing to try something new and give us their support.

Jim, CEO of Denver Water, whose rallying cry to be "the best water utility in the nation" inspired us to try to be the best internal audit team to match.

Stephanie Zayatz, writer of Denver-based fiction, who held my hand during the book writing process.

David, Lean Sensei, who showed astounding patience teaching me a better way.

STORY:

"The Toyota style is not to create results by working hard. It is a system that says there is no limit to people's creativity. People don't go to Toyota to 'work' they go there to 'think.'" – Taiichi Ohno

LIVING A **LEAN & AGILE** AUDIT

It's 7:30 Monday morning, and David, the Audit Manager, arrives at the office. Much of this large utility is made up of engineers and field workers, who tend to get working before the sun comes up. So, he comes in early because he thinks it appropriate that his Internal Audit team behave like their audit clients. In his opinion, it tends to build credibility.

His first stop is the Visual Control Board for his audit team. Right now, they're running one big audit; but the board can be rearranged to function for several audits at a time. The audit has entered the meat of the testing phase, and the team is working on its second Iteration or "Sprint." They often call them Sprints as an allusion to the IT Agile techniques borrowed to build this process, but they sometimes call them "chunks" or even "sections." It didn't really matter.

While he notes that the term Sprint is not entirely accurate, and trained IT Agile developers sometimes get confused by it, it easily jumps to his lips whenever talking about the next time-boxed portion of the audit. "Audit Sprints" weren't the same as "software development Sprints," but the term worked, so he kept using it. In casual conversation he often alternated between Sprint and Iteration. Probably confused people, but he couldn't break the habit.

A few years ago, the audit team had conspiratorially signed out a company pickup truck and gone off to a nearby home improvement store. They'd bought three sheets of 4'x8' melamine-coated fiberboard and snuck them in the side door. Melamine is the same stuff cheaper whiteboards are usually made of. The sheets had barely fit in the building's old elevators, but they'd managed to guide them into the Internal Audit space without being seen by the Facilities team, who might have questioned them.

On that day, Samir, a Senior Auditor, had along a cordless drill and with a great deal of adjusting and readjusting to get the sheets plumb and true, the audit team screwed them to the wall long-ways up. They'd created an entire wall that could be written on with dry erase markers. Together with a few screws, the whole thing cost less than $50.

This morning, the Audit Manager looks first at the center panel of the Visual Control Board. It's known as the Two-Week Panel and it shows what's on tap this week and next, conveyed by dozens of colored sticky notes.

David searches for his color, which is red.

At the beginning of the audit, during the opening Standup, he'd chosen red stickies. Samir had chosen green and Julia had chosen teal. Sara had found a strange hue of fuchsia that she liked.

Looking to the edge of the Two-Week Panel, David could see the other colors that had been selected by members of the client team. This was a human resources audit and the Talent Manager's color was blue and the Chief of HR had selected hot pink. There were, perhaps, another seven or eight other team members represented, their names written large on their chosen sticky color and arranged in a line. You could forget your color, so this was an easy reference.

They'd about run out of colors. The Audit Manager chuckled to himself, recalling the discussion in that opening Standup about what to call the representative from Legal's color. Was it "seafoam" or something else?

David liked his color because red was easy to spot.

Each colored sticky represented an activity that needed doing. As he was looking, he noted that the team had done a good job Friday afternoon closing out the previous week and resetting the board for the next two weeks. They'd shifted all the stickies to the left and written the dates of the next week in the boxes at the top.

He saw that there weren't many stickies in the later part of the second week and resisted the urge to get concerned. His team often chided him when he would remark, "Hey, looks like we're either done or taking next week off. Is that true?"

They'd remind him that they always met mid-morning on Monday to be sure the full two weeks were planned, and they would get annoyed with him if he jumped the gun and bugged them about it before then. They were nice about it, but they'd usually warn him that he'd better "chill" until at least Tuesday morning. David didn't care when they set their meeting to plan the next two weeks, so long as it got done.

He saw that today the audit team had assigned him to review Observations 15 and 21. There was a red sticky under Monday that told him that. Because it was under today, it told him that the audit team needed the review by the end of the day to stay on schedule. He also saw that there was a planning meeting for the next Sprint this week, which he needed to attend, and an important discussion of the observations they had from the last Iteration coming up in about three days.

"Ah, that's why they need my review today," he reasons.

It was a working agreement the team had defined at the beginning of this audit that the client would get at least two days to read and digest any observations before meeting about them. So, if the team were to honor that promise, they'd need to get these observations in their hands by tomorrow morning at the latest.

After studying his red colored stickies, he browses the other colors to get a sense of which auditors are doing what work and whether the workload balance seems reasonable.

He glances at the top of the Board, at the "Doghouse." The Doghouse is a taped off section of the Board where stickies that are behind schedule are put. Fortunately, today there is only one and it has to do with a data request the client is working on. He recalls that he'd heard during Friday's 15-minute Standup that it was taking a bit longer than expected to pull the data, but the prognosis was good for having it today. That sticky would stay there until the action was complete and the audit team received the data.

The sticky in the Doghouse was light yellow, denoting that Greg, the HR team's Data Analyst, owned the task. David knew that Greg hated when his colored stickies appeared in the Doghouse, so unless there was a real problem with the data, David felt certain the audit team would be getting the data soon. There would be an update at this afternoon's Standup and he could decide then whether he needed to get involved to expedite it.

David turned his attention to the Work Progress Panel of the Visual Control Board.

The audit team had easy access to a large format plotter in the nearby Engineering Division. So they'd used Microsoft Excel to create a grid that could be printed large – about 3'x4' – that showed the major pieces of the audit. This was the most common approach when they weren't auditing "on the road."

When the audit team was doing audit work primarily in another location, they would print all the Visual Control Board panels on more portable 11"x17" paper, but the bigger print was easier for folks to reference at Standups. This audit mostly involved people in the same building, so they went big.

For this audit, the Work Progress Panel shows all 55 Control Objectives arranged in subject groups. This audit is a pretty comprehensive "health check" of a variety of HR functions. There are eight subject groups – Compensation, Performance Management, Compliance, Employee Relations, and then three aspects of Talent Acquisition (Recruiting, Hiring, and Onboarding). The aspects of Talent Acquisition account for 25 of the 55 Control Objectives. The rest had between five and eight Control Objectives each.

Because HR had personnel teams for each of these subject groups, it had seemed simple to structure the Iterations around each personnel team. That made setting interviews easier, and you could tell whole groups of folks exactly when they would be needed. He recalled being thanked several times for that minor courtesy.

For each audit, they had to figure out the best way to structure the subject groups and define the Sprints. They were all different. It just depended on the risks they were auditing. This one seemed to be working fairly well.

David scans the sticky-sized Control Objective boxes to remind himself of the details this audit is covering. Each box has a single shorthand sentence describing the Control Objective and an Andon circle in the bottom right corner. The Andon, a Japanese term, is simply an easily recognized indicator of progress. Empty = no progress. Fully colored = everything complete.

Though similar in some ways to Agile "Burn-Down Charts," the Work Progress Panel owes more of its DNA to Lean Continuous Improvement techniques. It makes the complete set of work visible and provides a way for everyone to observe progress towards completion. Even the Chief of Staff can pop in and have a quick look if she wants to.

Out of the corner of his eye, David catches a glimpse of the Andon Key the team is using for this audit. Each colored sliver means something – e.g., fieldwork steps are done, workpapers are reviewed, observations issued, and so on.

It's easy to lose track, so someone had taped a printout of the Key where everyone could see it. That was a Lean thing. When in doubt, tape something on a wall.

The Work Progress Panel tells him that in the first Iteration of the audit they'd tackled all three aspects of Talent Acquisition. That had been a lot of work in one Iteration (about five weeks) and he made a mental note to ask, in the coming Retrospective, whether that had been too much for the audit team and the clients. He wasn't sure whether the client liked that much intensity all at once or would have preferred it broken up a bit. It could go either way. He shrugged and reminded himself, "We reserve the right to get better." That was also a Lean aphorism.

He sees from the Work Progress Panel that most of the work of the Talent Iteration is complete. Many of the top halves of the Andons are completely filled in black – meaning the testing has been completed, observations issued, and their accuracy confirmed with the client.

He notes two Andons where tiny slivers remain uncolored. That reminds him that he's not given final approval to those workpapers. And there is a purple checkmark in the corner of the box, which denotes that he's already given those workpapers a first review. They will need a second. That had been a pretty simple invention to help him keep track. But he might not do it in the next audit; he'd have to see.

During the first workpaper review, he'd asked several questions in the margins, which haven't yet been addressed, so he isn't comfortable approving them yet. He glances over at the Two-Week Panel and sees that his Audit Owner (like an auditor-in-charge) has a sticky note with a task to answer his questions by Thursday. "Looks good," he thinks, and he doesn't give the subject much more thought. It would either get done, or that sticky would move up to the Doghouse. Either way, it would be visible and would get attention.

The Work Progress Panel also tells him, in rough terms, that even though they'd only just completed Talent, and are just starting Compliance, they are nearly half way through the audit.

To the left of each group are stickies with date ranges. Compensation is marked for three weeks and the rest are only time-boxed for one- and two-week Sprints each. David knows that Compensation will be the heaviest lifting remaining. There are nine Control Objectives to test, and it might not fit into the three weeks allotted. But that chunk involves just one contact person in HR and a lot of data analysis work with Greg, the Data Analyst. Data analysis work always ends up being shorter than interviewing. And when the work involves the same few people, things go more quickly. You didn't have to spend the first 15 minutes of each meeting reintroducing the audit and getting folks to relax.

He also notes that several of the Control Objectives on the Work Progress Board have lines through them. That will shorten the work to come. The continual reassessment of risk and usefulness, which is a standard discussion point in the audit team's internal planning meetings, had concluded that there wasn't enough value (risk vs. effort) in continuing to test those sections.

In one such case, the client had offered, up front, that they weren't doing what the Control Objective described. So the team had jointly agreed to stop further work and write up the condition in an observation. No reason to waste everyone's time on something we'd all agreed wasn't happening. In other cases, when the amount of necessary test work was better understood and weighed against the risks involved, the audit team had asked permission from him to cut certain Control Objectives from testing. In most cases, he'd agreed.

"That was fine," he thought. After all, neither his team's time nor the client's time was inexhaustible or free – and the board wanted *reasonable* assurance, not *perfect* assurance.

Glancing again at the cancelled Control Objectives, he thought about the strength of the control environment they'd seen so far. While the audit team had written several observations, few of them seemed to indicate a serious lack of attentiveness by management. He'd been taught years ago as a young auditor that the question you were really asking in every audit was, "How does management know it's working, and how would they know if it stopped working?" He'd also been taught that assessing leadership quality is a fair part of any audit. So far, this HR management team seemed to have most of their bases covered, so cancelling some of these Control Objectives didn't seem to be particularly chancy.

He takes a moment to review the Master Calendar. As a tool, it seems so simple, yet it had saved his backside many times. The HR audit is expected to take three months, so this Master Calendar covers four. This is a long audit and, for a small one, the Master Calendar could just as easily cover only a few weeks. The Master Calendar is just four 11"x17" monthly printouts, with the weekends cut off, taped in sequence to one panel of the Visual Control Board. They are specific to this engagement and will be torn down when it's over.

He smiles as he remembers that at the beginning of the audit, the audit team and client team had marked when they were on vacation, at training, or otherwise engaged for at least a half-day. They'd done it with thin half-inch masking tape and a pen. Again, so simple, and so often overlooked.

He reviews the big milestones that are marked on the Master Calendar. Someone had found fanciful cloud- and star-shaped stickies, and these were used to denote big moments in the audit. There was a yellow star for when the final Iteration was expected to be done, a blue one for when the draft report was to be delivered, and a hot pink cloud for when the closeout party would be held.

He smiles at the notion of a closeout party and wonders if his audit colleagues at other companies ever drink fake champagne with their clients to celebrate successfully completing an audit.

Whenever he reviews the Master Calendar like this, he always recalls the scramble, more than a year ago, to launch an "emergency audit." The CEO had abrupted requested the work to start in March.

That was fine, except no one, it seemed, was in the office at the same time for the first six weeks of the audit. The combined audit and client teams had used a ton of thin masking tape to mark most of their staff out of the office across multiple weeks. The problem occurred because of week-long Spring Breaks in the various school districts that didn't align, running from March to the middle of April.

For that audit, if the combined team had not used the Master Calendar, there would have been no practical way to navigate those two months and get any audit work done.

He notices a potential problem visible on the Master Calendar and writes himself a red sticky. He places the sticky under today's date on the Two-

Week Panel, as a reminder to discuss it at the next Standup. He has a few vacation days planned right before the end of the last Iteration, when an important observation meeting would likely need to take place. If something didn't change, it seemed unlikely that he'll be able to give final sign-off on the observations and still give the client a couple of days to review. They'd need to figure a way around that.

The Master Calendar makes it obvious that, since that observation meeting is near the end of the audit, there won't be much ability to flex the schedule without bumping the targeted final completion date (and the closeout party). So, it probably means asking his auditors to work some extra hours, shifting work between them or to him, or setting up a plan where he takes the documents to review on the plane. Who knows? All he really knows is that they'd figure it out by asking the team.

Before he goes to his office to read emails and prepare for his morning meetings, he stops to look over the Hearts & Minds Panel of the Visual Control Board. It's a mess of stickies hovering above a dashed line that bisects the panel. His eye is drawn to the sticky that says, "Don't waste our time." It's nestled among stickies that read things like, "No surprises," "Process not People," "Keep it fun," "Assume positive intent," and "Keep listening and communicating."

He remembers the opening Standup. It would have been easy to have taken offense at the one about wasting time. Earlier in his career he probably would have. It could easily be taken as a dig at his whole profession and livelihood.

It had come from a curmudgeonly client team member, Albert, who was clearly not delighted to be told to come to a daily meeting to be audited.

Even so, it was an honest statement of what Albert wanted. And, in point of fact, it was a fair request. Even if it did have somewhat "grumpy" roots. At the moment, that sticky is above the line. That means the Single Combined Team had recently agreed we were all doing pretty well not wasting each other's time. Earlier in the audit, it had dropped just below the line. This was mostly during the planning stage, and several invited staff members who were regularly attending Standups weren't yet needed. They hadn't felt involved, and justly thought their time was being misused.

An obligation of the Hearts & Minds Panel is that if a sticky drops below the line, "Countermeasures" must be put in place to push it back up. In their case, the Single Combined Team had concluded that the staff members could shift their attendance to only two days a week until they were more needed. They weren't excused altogether, because then the group would have to get them up to speed later. But they could come less often. And those who were coming every day had committed to sharing important bits with them in the meantime. David is glad that nothing is currently below the line.

It had only taken him about 8 minutes to get up to speed, and he didn't have to pester any of his folks to do it. He pulls out his cellphone and takes a picture of the Visual Control Board. While that gives him a record of the audit on this date, he really does it so he won't have to get up and look again when he forgets what red stickies were assigned to him that day.

As he turns to go to his office, he recalls to himself how important the Hearts & Minds Panel has been to getting this unusually collaborative audit process off the ground. Sarcastically, he says to himself, "Who knew that paying attention to how people feel would make such a difference?" He smiles as he enters his office.

It would still be about 20 minutes before any of his auditors arrived for work. Julia is usually the earliest. She lives north of town where traffic is worst, so she routinely gets an early start.

He sits down and begins reading emails.

After about his sixteenth email, David looks up. It had just occurred to him what he hadn't been spending his time on this morning, because of the new audit process they'd been running. He realizes he hasn't been putting out fires borne out of misunderstandings and hasn't been sending griping emails that simultaneously demand and beg for information from his audit clients. And he hasn't been sending inquiries to his staff asking when things will be done so he can feel "in the loop." Instead, he's been doing real productive work. Work that advances knowledge and insight. Work worth paying for.

It strikes him how different the last two years have been from the first 15 of his career in auditing. Every year of that time he'd either read articles in journals or gone to conferences where authors and speakers would encourage the profession to partner better with management, to do more with less, and to be more flexible. Folks would have tips and tricks, and some success stories; but for a profession devoted to making things better, he reflects, we sure haven't figured out how to "take our own medicine." How can we all still be talking about this? We'd never put up with that kind of response from an audit client.

"The old way," he says, shaking his head. The old way was just so wasteful and rigid. More than that, it reeked of arrogance. To assume that we fully understood someone else's environment so well, that after briefly studying it we could lay out an entire unmovable audit program just screamed conceit.

Somehow we imagined the clients wouldn't notice that conceit. No wonder we auditors always get portrayed as imperious turkeys in movies. We kind of deserve it. And yet we can't understand why no one wants to partner with us. With a small grimace to himself and a hope that maybe, in time, some of what his team has learned to do might seep into the rest of the profession, he returns to his emails. Only half a page more of them to go.

His auditors arrive in the office, and for a bit he can hear them laying out the full two weeks of activities, writing stickies, and discussing sequencing. They evidently turn to doing analytical test work or documenting workpapers for a while, because they become quiet. A few hours later he sees them pass his office with folios and pens in hand. He recalls, from his quick review of the Visual Control Board that morning, that they have an interview today with the HR manager in charge of Compensation, where they will seek to learn about her processes and what must go right every day for her to be successful.

David turns back to reviewing Observations 15 and 21, pulling up the supporting workpapers on his left-hand screen and putting the observations on the right. It is important to him that by today's 2:00 Standup, he can color in the Andon on the sticky he was assigned. As the boss, he never wants to be the bottleneck.

The team needs it today, and he always gets a silly rush when he can color in his stickies – whether by himself or in front of a group. Lean trainers have described it as a "serotonin rush," and say that everyone gets it as part of a feeling of accomplishment. He'd heard some people refer to it as the "whoosh." He thinks to himself that it seems an oddly human thing for an auditor to experience – after all, most people don't think auditors feel at all.

It's 1:55, and there are voices in the hall coming this way. That will be the HR staff coming to today's Standup. For this audit, Legal usually sends an employment attorney to help interpret potential compliance issues and answer questions around what the law requires. He hears her voice and knows she is in the bunch as well. She's the one with the seafoam sticky color.

It had been a running joke that Standups must start exactly on time. As much as participants may not love coming, they really hated being late and even worse to appear late because the meeting started two minutes early. So the audit team had been told in no uncertain terms never to start even 30 seconds early. There is a sticky on the Hearts & Minds Panel that says, "Don't Start Early."

While mildly humorous, what that demand really did was sanction a few minutes of casual chit-chat among the audit and client teams about what they did over the weekend, the vacation they just came back from, or whatever. Being Monday, and folks being early, there is a bit of that today. It is sort of odd how valuable this casual time is. Everyone becomes more human.

At precisely 2:00, Samir takes the lead and begins "working the Board." As David had done that morning, Samir starts with the Two-Week Panel, including the Doghouse. Folks who have completed tasks are handed markers and encouraged to come forward and ceremoniously fill in their Andons. They get to enjoy the serotonin rush. David is delighted to be one of them. He fills in the Andon on the sticky that tasked him with reviewing Observations 15 and 21. His team knows that those observation sheets are ready to go.

The stickies that remain incomplete, some for today, but most for the next several days, are talked about briefly. Are they on track? Does everyone understand the task? Any obstacles?

Greg gives an update on the data request sticky that's in the Doghouse. The report had errored out twice, but he'd reset the parameters and thinks it's working now. He promises delivery before end of day. He jokingly asks if he could fill in the Andon based on that promise and the group "pooh-poohs" him, just as he knew they would. He'll have to wait for his serotonin.

Samir shifts attention to the Work Progress Panel and updates everyone on progress so far – based on more slivers being filled in black. One of the HR team steps forward and takes a picture of the Panel. He's keeping an identical Panel updated down in the HR suite. He says it helps everyone stay focused on getting the audit done on time. "My colleagues will walk by it a dozen times a day, so there will be no excuse not knowing the status," he's said in the past.

Samir points out on the Panel which Iteration is next. It's going to be Compensation, and the Compensation Manager points out that he's gone for a week, in two weeks. He explains that it would be better for him if any interviews got scheduled in the next several days. Everyone glances at the Master Calendar, and sure enough - his vacation is marked there. The audit team just missed it. Or at least they missed how it would likely affect scheduling.

That's okay.

An audit of this size, with a dozen-plus key client contacts, is a complex mass of moving parts. It's likely that such conflicts will arise. The system is designed to make them visible so they can be dealt with.

Sensing there isn't anything else that needs discussion on the Work Progress Panel, Samir uses the Compensation Manager's comment to pivot the group to review the Master Calendar. He asks if everyone has their out-of-office time marked accurately. One of the HR Compliance folks mentions that she will no longer be off next Friday but expects to be out the last week of the audit for a conference. That doesn't affect much now, but it needs to be recorded. Julia hands her a roll of thin masking tape and a marker, so she can make the change on the Master Calendar.

Based on the reminder sticky he wrote earlier; David takes that moment to mention that he foresees a conflict with his vacation days and his ability to approve the final set of observations in time for the last observation meeting. As he brings it up, he walks over and fills in the Andon and peels the reminder sticky off the wall, putting it in the "completed" pile. The reminder has done its job. Samir, who is facilitating the Standup, acknowledges the issue and smartly tells the group that the audit team will discuss the conflict offline. So long as it can be resolved, it really only impacts them.

Most of the Single Combined Team are present today. All of the auditors are at the Standup, and only one or two members of the HR team are missing. So Samir decides it's a good day to review the Hearts & Minds Panel.

As Samir turns the group's attention to that panel, David recalls how tense it was at the beginning of the audit getting the two teams to come out of their protective shells and offer their thoughts. Trust hadn't yet been built. Most of them had stood with crossed arms, wishing they were somewhere else and weren't being audited. To get the group started, David had written three or four statements that mattered to him and placed the stickies on the panel. Then one person from HR stepped forward, and then another. By now, there are about a dozen statements on the panel.

Samir takes each in turn and asks the group, "How are we at this?" "Should we move it up or down?" "Above the line or below?"

Here at the middle of the audit, the audit team and client team are working pretty well together, so nothing drops below the line and a couple of stickies even get moved up. Someone points out that the mood is much more fun than they'd ever expected, and they really appreciate that. So, the sticky that says, "Keep it fun" gets moved up a couple of inches. Samir finishes this part of the Standup, with about three minutes left of the allotted fifteen, by asking if any new stickies need to be added to the Hearts & Minds Panel. No one has any, so he quickly moves on to the final portion of the Standup, known as "Going Around the Room."

Samir starts with the person on his left in the half-circle (it was his right on Friday). Do they have anything for the group? The first person doesn't, but the second person offers that they could avoid a scheduled interview next week, if they and one of the auditors could meet briefly right following this Standup. The offer is accepted, and they agree to get together immediately following. Samir continues.

Having gone completely around the half-circle, Samir declares the Standup over and remarks that he's only one minute over time today. Several folks chide him about it. Another good chuckle for all.

As the participants head back to their workspaces, snagging pieces of fudge that had been brought in by one of the auditors, Samir marks attendance on a chart they'd taped to the wall for that purpose.

Noticing this, David reflects that at the beginning of the audit, there had been some issues with HR staff regularly showing up to Standups, but not the HR managers. In our old way of auditing, the traditional way, that kind of thing was usually handled in grumpy generalities (e.g., griping that "so-and-so never shows up"). But Lean teaches that if it's important, measure it. Accordingly, the audit team crafted a red-green attendance chart and began marking who showed up each day.

Attendance improved.

Though David had also asked the Chief of HR to push her managers to show up more routinely, it mostly seemed that the act of measuring accounted for the better attendance.

He recalls that it hadn't hurt when he had given away a $10 fast food gift card as a prize for best attendance through the first half of the audit. It amuses him to think that none of his audit colleagues at other companies had likely done that before.

David waits for a moment to see if anyone needs him and then goes back to his office.

He's been fully briefed. It took 15 minutes, and he knows exactly the status of this audit. He knows from the Visual Control Board what his team needs from him today and roughly for the next two weeks. Tomorrow, he and his auditors will meet in their own Standup to talk about issues and obstacles, and to get his input and direction. He feels engaged and on top of the audit, while at the same time respecting his people to do what they do best.

A Word about Terminology

This book has a glossary, and you can cross-reference meanings there.

However, more importantly, we want to state up front that we frequently use Agile IT terms in broad conceptual ways in this book. True experts in Agile Software Development and, especially, "Scaled Agile" will likely find this practice infuriating. We don't intend to be true to the details of these methodologies. We're auditors, not software developers.

Instead, we are shamelessly stealing ideas, at their most conceptual level, from Agile development, Lean, and the Toyota Production System. We expect to mischaracterize them in their natural state to some degree. As one immediate example, we will use the terms Scrum and Agile essentially interchangeably. And, while we fully understand that to the purest practitioner there are crucial differences – to an auditor who is borrowing them as conceptual building blocks – the differences are not meaningful.

We also know that while there are entities that certify people as Scrum Masters and Green/Black Belts, which suggests there is a "right way to do it," the truth is every organization in practice does these things differently.

Moreover, neither approach suggests that they are rigid methodologies. Instead, they call themselves "frameworks," and they encourage their practitioners to use the principles and thinking to do what makes most sense for their organizations.

Finally, the techniques in this book are described primarily from an operational "assurance" audit context. That's where they were invented. Nevertheless, we see no reason they shouldn't be exportable to financial, compliance, and consulting work, at least in some form.

Active Auditing

We have coined the term "Active Auditing" to describe the integrated system we're about to teach because it is, by far, the best descriptor.

It's not fancy or kitschy, but it's dead-on accurate. We thought about calling it "Nimble Auditing" or "Open Auditing." Both would be reasonable labels to hang on the system. The process you will learn in the coming pages is certainly nimble, and it demands a level of openness from both the auditors and clients that is seldom seen in our profession.

However, what the system does best is drive everyone connected to an audit to become active contributors, central players in an important project for their board. There is motion and interaction well beyond most traditional audit work. "Active" is the antonym for "passive" and it's the opposite of "waiting," which is the primary Lean Waste we attack with the Active Audit system.

Active Audits can be fun, while still being hard-nosed and value-added. There is nothing in Active Auditing that suggests less than pure independence and biting objectivity. Active Auditing is not weak and it doesn't let issues "off the hook."

Strap in, and let's explore it..

ONE

"Great things in business are never done by one person.
They're done by a team of people." – Steve Jobs

THE CASE FOR AUDITING AGILE-ISHLY

This book is mostly about how to <u>do</u> something, but we'll take a few moments to describe <u>why</u> it's worth doing.

We built this approach primarily out of frustration with how audits were working, but also partly because we were in an organization that had committed to a Lean journey and we didn't want to be left out.

Audits were taking too long and were too often ending up in conflicts, frequently just as we approached the report publishing phase.

Initially, we thought the problem was that we hadn't explained the audit process well enough or often enough.

There was a sliver of truth in that and it seemed like something we could fix. After all, while we'd studiously laid out the audit process way back at the beginning of the engagement during the entrance meeting, we didn't reinforce it all that much later in the audit. It probably was unreasonable to expect our clients to remember how it worked eight weeks later, even though we'd showed them some pretty nifty diagrams at the start. Maybe just covering the information again at mid-audit would help. We tried. Didn't help.

Giving that a go more than once, we began to realize that there was no way to "explain ourselves" better. No matter how fancy we made our audit process diagrams (and we did some really slick ones) and how diligently we stuck to our entrance meeting scripts and checklists, the clients couldn't hear us.

We then began to study our audit process, looking for ways to improve it. We process-mapped it using Lean techniques, but while we could always do better, we kept sensing that the process steps weren't the problem.

The more we thought about it, the more we began to realize that the central problem was that the audit clients (we never called them "auditees") weren't as invested in completing the audit as we were. We got measured on whether we completed the annual audit plan, but they didn't. We weren't equally working toward a common outcome.

In their masterwork, *Crucial Conversations: Tools for Talking when Stakes are High*, Patterson, Grenny, McMillan, and Switzer call this "mutual purpose" and they describe that to succeed in interactions, one has to really care about the interests of others and not just our own; and we must be comfortable that they care about ours.

We'll reference Crucial Conversations several times in this book, because its concepts are so important to the success of Active Auditing. We strongly recommend any audit leader who intends to shift to an Active Audit approach read their book and, if possible, receive training in Crucial Conversations.

The realization that, fundamentally, in traditionally-run audits we didn't have mutual purpose with our clients, was central to the development of Active Auditing.

To deal with this, we began to analyze exact behaviors of our clients and ourselves. And we tried to do so dispassionately, stepping outside the traditional dynamic of auditor vs. auditee, to imagine a mutual purpose and what that would mean to the way we did our audits.

Crucial Conversations teaches that when the stakes are high, an effective strategy is to actively "explore others' paths." So, we did.

Auditors are great at interviewing and absorbing information, but, be honest, we usually do so from the other side of a pane of glass – as though the interviewees are animals in a zoo. We find their activities fascinating, but they are divorced from our own. Studying the dynamics between the client and the auditors required us to break that glass, which wasn't as easy as it sounds.

Our first "aha" moment was when we grasped that, contrary to all previously understood and normal auditor thinking, the audit clients didn't really want the audit to be over quickly. That was a stunning realization, and I expect some readers would argue with me over it.

There is no doubt that nine of ten audit clients would prefer the audit to never have happened, but once it commences, there are very legitimate reasons to not have it come to a close rapidly. And, by the way, I'm not really suggesting that audit clients think about this stuff cognitively. Rather, the following reasons just affect their sense of urgency relative to the audit:

It's in da past - The longer it takes for the audit report to be published, the further in the past the events contained in it will appear. This reason is rooted in the fear that management of the audited area will be blamed for any findings. If they can argue that the audit covered data from a long time ago, they can argue that it's all in the past and doesn't really count now. It's even possible, they sometimes think, to delay so long that the report never comes out, or if it does, it never gets read by anyone important.

I can fix it - If the audit drags out, they have a greater chance of fixing issues before the report is published. This helps them appear in control of their area and this is better than just committing to fix an issue in the future.

Understand me - Many clients desperately want to be understood by their auditors, so they are inclined to invite the auditors to spend sufficient time understanding every side of their business. While this flies in the face of the classic stories about keeping auditors in the dark and ushering us out the door quickly; outside of investigations, I've found it to be a very real behavior.

As further support, I offer the primary client complaint. In my experience, it's almost universal that, when displeased clients are surveyed, they say the auditors didn't understand their business well enough to issue the findings they did. Or, worse, the auditors mischaracterized what was important.

For years, in teams I've run, we've surveyed our clients with post-audit feedback forms. That data told us that failing to understand their business was nearly every unhappy client's chief complaint. Additionally, I'd talk to other chief audit executives at conferences and roundtables, where I'd hear this same complaint repeated. Initially, I assumed it meant my auditors weren't very good at seeing the client's point of view. In later years, I assumed that in most cases it was merely a natural human protective technique, intended to diminish the credibility of the findings – even if just in the client's own mind. However, when we asked them honestly, we found it isn't a dodge at all. It's what really concerns them.

From the client's standpoint, the greatest sin an auditor can commit is to write an observation or finding that is flawed because the auditor didn't spend enough time understanding things from the client's perspective.

Consequently, in many cases, "shooing" the audit team out too quickly is scarier than having us hang around.

Low grade irritant - Finally, and perhaps most importantly, while having auditors consume your time and that of your staff is irritating, on balance it's usually a fairly low-grade irritant compared with all the other priorities in the client's world. Sure, we might be taking up one of their conference rooms, but we usually end up like a "buzzing noise," just under awareness.

So, faced with getting an important report out on time or satisfying the requests of the internal auditors, they usually focus on the report.

By the way, from experience, this behavior seems to occur just as frequently, if not more, with travelling audits. Though audit managers complain if the audit team didn't get everything it needed from a trip to the field, eventually the audit team is forced to head back to headquarters and the whole thing continues over email. At this point, for travelling audits you are now out of their space, the buzzing noise has abated and yet the audit lingers on. Since internal auditors are usually considered part of overhead, to the client, this behavior doesn't seem to cost anything.

These aren't sinister reasons, they're just very human. And they help explain the Mutual Purpose Gap that exists between auditors and their clients. I've known some auditors to try to close this gap through fear. They reason that if the auditors are viewed as scary people, the clients will fall in line and be more responsive.

Few do, but many "appear" to. And, while it seems every issue of *Internal Auditor* magazine contains some story about how to be viewed as partners with the business, this behavior persists. Indeed, the continued existence of those articles proves it.

So, the question becomes, "What can auditors do to close the Mutual Purpose Gap?" How can they influence their clients to be equally invested in having constructive, insightful audits that complete on schedule? We found employing the Active Auditing system goes a long way towards shrinking that gap.

Mother of Invention

In our organization, our frustration collided with a sudden need to get a particularly hefty audit done in a short time.

The organization had been overhauling its financial and budgetary governance processes for several years. This included a ground-up reimplementation of its primary enterprise resource planning (ERP) system, which among other things, intended to get its budget system on the same chart of accounts as its accounting system. No small effort.

The work had been completed, along with a tremendous amount of associated financial process reengineering. So the CEO asked us to swap out several audits from the annual audit plan with a "capstone audit" to see if the extensive changes had resulted in sufficiently better controls and governance. It mattered to him specifically because a clean bill of health around the organization's financial controls would help his efforts to request an appropriate increase in spending authority. Such an increase would likely result in significant efficiencies for the organization's leadership.

To provide the requested assurance, the scope of the audit would need to include 75 Control Objectives. We'll discuss Control Objectives more later, but for now it's enough to understand that verifying that each of the 75 Control Objectives had been achieved would require about three "normally sized" audits' worth of fieldwork.

Essentially, we needed to find a way to cram three audits in the space of one. And the requirement was that it complete by year-end, or shortly after. This period covered both Thanksgiving and Christmas, and in our organization most people took substantial amounts of vacation time during both periods.

The task seemed impossible, so the time had come to shake things up.

We had on our hands what Lean calls a "burning platform."

Burning Platform

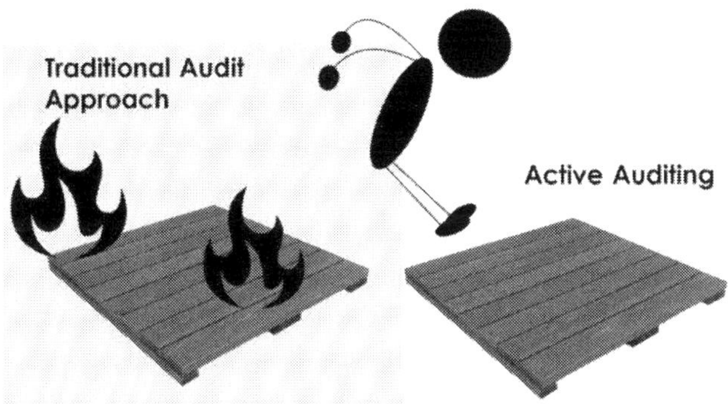

The platform is said to be "burning" because it's no longer a safe place to stand. We had to jump. We were compelled to develop an audit process that would address the Mutual Purpose Gap and allow us to meet the work objective.

Data Driven

The final piece of the puzzle was an analysis we'd done of the last four years of our audit work. The analysis calculated the cycle times in days between each key step of the audit. It was based on data from a manually-kept approval log that stored dates of completion alongside the manager's initials. If we'd had an automated workpapers system, we might have been able to get the information from there, but we didn't.

From these log entries, we could calculate how long each step of the last 48 months of audits had taken. We knew the elapsed time between the entrance meeting and the delivery of the final report, between the issuance of observations and agreement on those observations, and even how long it typically took clients to review drafts of our reports for accuracy prior to publishing. The analysis tracked about a dozen important process steps and calculated mean and median cycle times for each.

That data told us that only about 33% of each audit was "active" fieldwork (e.g., auditors aggressively engaged in testing analysis, interviews, writing, and documenting). The rest was waiting – waiting for document requests, waiting to hold an interview, waiting for answers to follow-up questions, waiting for observations to be reviewed, and waiting for reports to be commented upon.

"Waiting" is one of the classic eight Lean Wastes, and Lean teaches that by making waste visible you can take steps to eliminate it.

So, we had our key.

We needed a way to make all that wait time visible to both the audit team and the clients, as it was happening, so we could attack it. Fortunately, theoretically, with a 1-3 ratio, if we could drive the accumulated wait time to zero, we'd have a chance of getting three audits' worth of work done in the time it usually took to do one.

This gave us a starting place.

Now the question shifted to, "What could we do to close the Mutual Purpose Gap and drive out the excessive wait time?"

If we could figure a way to do both, we'd get off the platform that was burning and on to one that was sustainable. Along the way, maybe some other things would get better too.

The Mashup

The components of a potential solution had been at hand for several years. And though we'd considered employing them before – the pressure of needing to get this sizeable audit done, coupled with the desire to fundamentally change the operating relationship between Internal Audit (IA) and its clients, drove us to actively mash them together for the first time.

Several years before, the audit team had conducted a deep System Development Life Cycle (SDLC) audit in the IT Division. Since the IT organization had committed to a Scrum development model, we'd gone to training, read books, and immersed ourselves thoroughly in Agile. We weren't experts, but in addition to giving us the tools to conduct the audit, we'd taken away key concepts that seemed portable to auditing.

As an IA team, we'd talk about them from time-to-time but had never gotten around to intentionally employing them.

Additionally, our organization had, for several years, been on a committed "Lean journey" of continuous improvement. Management stood up an eight-person Lean Office, led by an experienced former Lean / Toyota Production System consultant, and that group was moving through the organization a piece at a time changing business process and spreading Lean culture.

IA had been early champions of the organization's Lean journey and worked closely with the Lean Office. Routinely, members of the audit team were included in Rapid Improvement Events as "fresh eyes." Our work would often be used at the beginning of Lean "Value Stream" efforts so that the leaders could decide where to begin improving. Several auditors even became trained Lean facilitators, filling in and leading Lean events two or three times a year. From this work, we knew the principles of Lean well.

The solution was to borrow pieces from both methodologies and "mash" them together to create a new methodology specifically for internal auditing, with a new combined set of principles.

So in 2017 Active Auditing was born in a small audit team in an important, yet regional, water utility. Innovation often happens in small places first… then expands. So it is here.

The Big Ideas

Active Auditing rests on three central pillars and incorporates five crucial supporting concepts, all created from the mashup of Agile and Lean. It also incorporates the fundamental flexibility to adjust as needed, which both Agile and Lean teach. The central pillars are:

1. Energetic Collaboration
2. Iterative Audit Execution
3. Visual Management

The crucial supporting concepts are:

- A3 Language & Thinking
- Gemba-Based Planning
- Experimentation

- Celebrations & Retrospectives
- Objectives-Based Risk Assessment

We use the three central pillars constantly. Whenever there is a decision to be made, we ask how we can make it with Energetic Collaboration, iteratively, and/or visually. The pillars are at the center of everything we do in an Active Audit.

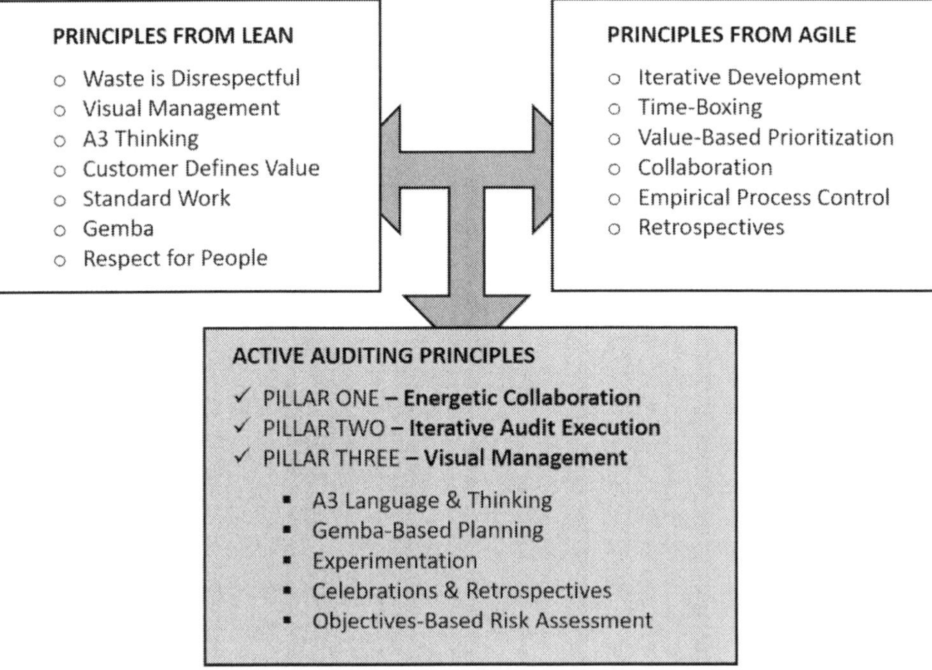

If we need to do a risk assessment as part of pre-engagement planning, how can I accomplish that using the pillars? Can I bring the clients into the risk assessment discussion? Can I think of the risk assessment not being done once at the beginning of the audit, but multiple times through the engagement, building on what's been learned? Can I conduct the risk assessment so that it makes the most important potential issues visible, not just to me, but to the clients as well?

The beauty of Lean and Agile is that they are ways of thinking, and not just techniques.

Lean teaches that no one's idea is better than another's unless we put a stop-watch (or whatever measuring tool is appropriate) and test it against the current state. We experiment and decide the best way we know how. Then we run with that until we think of a better way and prove it is better.

That's how Active Auditing works.

In the following sections, we'll describe ways to tackle the most common activities in internal auditing in Lean & Agile ways using the three central pillars and the five crucial supporting concepts.

Requisite Agile

According to the lore of Agile and Scrum, it was a group of self-described "software rebels," a.k.a. "developer anarchists," who drafted the first Agile Manifesto during a get-together at Snowbird, Utah in 2001.

The Manifesto was a sort of "Declaration of Independence" from the old way of running software projects. That group called themselves the Agile Alliance. The Agile Alliance has grown from its original 17 members and has continued to spread the "religion" of Agile ever since.

While Amazon.com lists over 2000 books related to Agile project management, the roots are in the Agile Manifesto and the 12 Agile Principles.

The Agile Manifesto

"We are uncovering better ways of developing software by doing it and helping others do it. Through this work we have come to value:

- **Individuals and interactions** over processes and tools
- **Working software** over comprehensive documentation
- **Customer collaboration** over contract negotiation
- **Responding to change** over following a plan

That is, while there is value in the items on the right, we value the items on the left more."

12 Agile Principles

"The following principles are based on the Agile Manifesto.

1. Our highest priority is to satisfy the customer through early and continuous delivery of valuable software.

2. Welcome changing requirements, even late in development. Agile processes harness change for the customer's competitive advantage.

3. Deliver working software frequently, from a couple of weeks to a couple of months, with a preference to the shorter timescale.

4. Business people and developers must work together daily throughout the project.

5. Build projects around motivated individuals. Give them the environment and support they need, and trust them to get the job done.

6. The most efficient and effective method of conveying information to and within a development team is face-to-face conversation.

7. Working software is the primary measure of progress.

8. Agile processes promote sustainable development. The sponsors, developers, and users should be able to maintain a constant pace indefinitely.

9. Continuous attention to technical excellence and good design enhances agility.

10. Simplicity--the art of maximizing the amount of work not done-- is essential.

11. The best architectures, requirements, and designs emerge from self-organizing teams.

12. At regular intervals, the team reflects on how to become more effective, then tunes and adjusts its behavior accordingly."

Requisite Lean

There is no Lean-specific moment of discovery equivalent to the anarchists in Snowbird. Rather, Lean derives from the Toyota Production System, which is a century or more in the making. It's not an acronym, it just means what it says – become leaner, scrappier, and more efficient.

It starts with ideas from Henry Ford, passes through WWII and the need to produce an exceptional amount in a short period of time, takes much along the way from W. Edwards Deming and Joseph Juran, and continues to the Toyota Motor Company. The heroes of the Toyota Production System are usually considered to be Taiichi Ohno and Shigeo Shingo. Today, the Shingo Institute and its Shingo Prize represent the pinnacle of Lean thinking.

There is not a single set of Lean Principles. But there are commonly drawn-upon principles, which form the basis of Active Auditing.

15 Common Lean Principles

1. Waste is disrespectful
2. Drive out No-Value Added (NVA) work
3. Employ "pull" systems, rather than "push" to prevent overproduction
4. Set for continuous flow
5. Even out the workload, eliminate "rushing forward and waiting"
6. Make it okay to stop the process to fix problems
7. Standard work – the best way we all know how right now
8. Visual Management
9. Proven technologies over new technologies – simple & manual over digital & complex
10. Gemba – go to where the work is done and open your eyes
11. The people involved must solve their own problems – it is disrespectful for others to impose solutions
12. Reflect and reassess, get better constantly
13. Unqualified respect for people
14. A3 Thinking – using a language of continuous improvement – e.g., Reason for Action, Current State, Target State, Gap Analysis, Solutions Approach, Experiments, Completion Plans, Confirmed State, and Insights – and getting it on a single page.
15. Customer defines value

Muda, Mura, & Muri

Expanding on the above common principles, it's useful to understand the concepts of Muda, Mura, and Muri. These Japanese terms are often referred to as the "Three Ms" of the Toyota Production System, and they represent bad management practices Lean organizations seek to eliminate.

Muda – Non-value-added (NVA) processes or "wastes." Some NVA is required, or necessary for the moment, perhaps because of regulation. This is often called Type One Muda. In contrast, Type Two Muda can be addressed by applying Lean principles and techniques.

Type Two Muda is frequently simplified into Lean's 8 Wastes. And clever writers have adopted the mnemonic of D-O-W-N-T-I-M-E to make the 8 Wastes easy to remember:

1. **D-Defects** – mistakes, errors, and scrap that require resources and rework to correct
2. **O-Overproduction** – producing more than is needed or before it is needed
3. **W-Waiting** – time lost or attention diverted while waiting for a previous process step to complete
4. **N-Non-Utilized Human Talent** – disrespecting people by under-utilizing them
5. **T-Transport** – unnecessary movement of product or material
6. **I-Inventory** – materials, product, or even information sitting and not being processed or utilized
7. **M-Motion** – unnecessary people motion (e.g., walking, hunting for things, reeducating and refreshing understanding)
8. **E-Extra-processing** – performing more work than is necessary to meet the customer's needs

Sometimes an "S" is added to the 8 Wastes to make DOWNTIMES.

9. **S-Safety** – disrespecting people by allowing unsafe conditions

Mura – Unevenness or irregularity in workflow. This kind of unevenness results in starting and stopping. Processes that gyrate in this way tend to cost more to maintain, as staffing and equipment is added to deal with peak demand, which then may sit idle in times of lower demand.

Muri – Overburdening people and processes by requiring them to run at a faster or longer pace than they should. It refers to "burning out" your system to achieve short term results, often then idling that system or underutilizing it in the next period. It is a sin in Lean to solve your throughput problem by asking the worker to "turn the wrench faster."

A3 Thinking

An A3 is simply the largest piece of paper, in European sizing, that an average Japanese manager can fit in an average Japanese fax machine. What's important is what's on that paper and the thinking behind it.

A3 Thinking is the art of getting everything we need to know about an important action on a single structured page. A classic Lean A3 is broken into nine boxes on what is essentially an 11"x17" piece of paper.

An A3 is a tool to manage change. It is used at a very strategic level, to plan and execute entire Value Stream efforts, spanning a wide variety of processes, and at tactical levels to manage single projects or Rapid Improvement Events.

An A3 starts by describing why the effort is necessary. Then it captures the current state. This is done, as much as possible, using metrics and not just anecdotes.

A3 Components

1) Reason for Action (the Why)	4) Gap Analysis	7) Completion Plans
Narrative	Problem / Root Cause	Action / Who / When / Status
2) Current State	5) Solutions Approach	8) Confirmed State
Narrative – Written & Pictorial; Metric / Current	If we.... / Then we expect...	Metric / Initial / Target / 30 / 90 / 1YR
3) Target State	6) Rapid Experiments	9) Insights
Narrative – Written & Pictorial; Metric / Target	Action / Expected Outcome / Actual Outcome	Learn / Feel / Take Away & Do

We developed an A3 when we set off to change our audit process, which resulted ultimately in Active Auditing. Along with a descriptive narrative, our current state described a series of metrics having to do with cycle time and wait time. As you may recall, we calculated that only about 30-33% of elapsed time in an audit was value-added audit work. That meant roughly 70% was wait time and other Non-Value-Added (NVA) time.

Our Target State included both an intended 50% reduction in NVA and descriptors that included – "Audit clients are as invested in the outcome of the audit as we are" and "We don't get into fights with clients as often."

You might think that 50% improvement is ridiculous. Perhaps something more reasonable like 15% would be more attainable.

You'd be wrong.

Lean teaches that until a business process (and auditing just another business process) has been subjected to continuous improvement attention five times, you should start by aiming to "half the bad and double the good." Elsewhere in our organization, we routinely saw 60% improvement, so 50% for us was entirely in-bounds and we needed to start somewhere.

Point of fact, on our first Active Audit, even fumbling through creating these techniques, we achieved roughly 66% improvement in cycle time and 95% improvement in mutual purpose.

We did so by A3 Thinking. We identified the gap between our current state and our target state. We imagined several approaches that might improve the situation. We experimented. Ultimately, we achieved the confirmed state you see described in this book. Along the way we learned a great deal about ourselves, much of which is described in the next chapter.

Active Audit Resources

Entire small-town libraries can be filled with books on Agile, Lean, auditing, and good leadership. We suggest a few for those who want to better understand the heritage of Active Auditing.

- Jeffrey K. Liker (2003). ***The Toyota Way: 14 Management Principles from the World's Greatest Manufacturer.*** New York: McGraw Hill Professional

- Taiichi Ohno, Norman Bodek (1988). ***Toyota Production System: Beyond Large-Scale Production.*** Portland, OR: Productivity, Inc.

- Ken Miller (2006). ***We Don't Make Widgets: Overcoming the Myths That Keep Government From Radically Improving.*** Governing Books.

- Chris Sims, Hillary Louise Johnson (2011). ***The Elements of Scrum.*** Foster City, CA: Dymaxicon

- Kerry Patterson, Joseph Grenny, Ron McMillan, Al Switzler (2012). ***Crucial Conversations: Tools For Talking When Stakes Are High.*** New York: McGraw-Hill.

- The Arbinger Institute (2009). ***Leadership and Self-Deception: Getting Out of the Box.*** ReadHowYouWant.

- K. Reding, P. Sobel, U. Anderson, M. Head, S. Ramamoorti, M. Salamasick, & C. Riddle (2015). ***Internal Auditing: Assurance & Advisory Services.*** Altamonte Springs, FL: The IIA Research Foundation.

TWO

"Nobody cares how much you know,
until they know how much you care."
– Theodore Roosevelt

PILLAR ONE: **ENERGETIC COLLABORATION**

It has been my experience that many auditors see the "professional independence line," the line auditors can't cross between their role and management's, as a fence line that separates them from their clients. Many even seem to take comfort in building that fence high and strong, perhaps to provide cover and perhaps because it helps those of us who are introverts from having to engage closely with those we are studying. I've even had auditors tell me their standards require them to be distant. But to conduct Active Audits, we've got to develop an energetically collaborative mindset. One that enthusiastically and genuinely seeks to partner with our clients.

We describe it as "energetic" for two reasons.

First, auditors have a tendency to be more comfortable with their laptops than with talking to their clients. So, think of this pillar in terms, not just of communicating to find mutual purpose, but aggressively hunting for opportunities to communicate.

Second, decades of experience with traditional auditors has taught clients not to accept offers of "we're from audit, we're here to help." Therefore, in our experience, taking our enthusiasm for collaboration a step "too far" on a regular basis is necessary to shake up this status quo. As we developed this methodology, we broke molds every chance we got – employing any technique we could to demonstrate we were on the same team.

Funnily, the most effective of these was a particular recipe of rice crispy treats.

By the way, we call them "clients" on purpose – because it reminds us we are working with them, not on them.

All of that said, we found developing a collaborative mindset to be the hardest of the three pillars to put in practice with auditors. To clarify, by "collaborative mindset" we mean the habit of, or predisposition, to want to collaborate and be open with audit clients.

It's not clear where young auditors pick up the skill of keeping their cards close to their vest. I can't recall any training sessions for new auditors that taught me to be circumspect about what was in the audit program, to hide what we were "really" asking about in our interviews, or to adopt a demeanor that broadcasts, "Hey I'm the one asking the questions here." But I, and most of the auditors I know, have a base tendency to approach audit work that way. Not exactly secretively, but certainly not in an overly forthcoming manner.

No doubt some of it comes from training to conduct investigations, where often the auditor really does need to withhold information from the subjects being interviewed either as a tactic, or purely because they don't have a need to know.

I'm not saying there aren't specific types of audits that need to be done in at least a partially non-collaborative manner. "Red Team" security audits come to mind. But even there, it's customary that some members of management are brought in on the work – even if it's just to calm panicking security techs or to prevent the White Hat hackers from damaging something important.

But outside of such settings, it's hard to argue that disclosing the details of the audit program and the associated fieldwork steps is a natural inclination for most auditors.

Yet, somehow, we've been taught to be enigmatic.

I know some of us have been burned by clients who clean up their house just before we arrive. I can recall audits in an insurance company, where we'd announce a claim office audit and overnight the Claim Adjusters would go into their tracking systems and "bump" every claim assigned to them. That way the claim file would appear to have been recently worked. They assumed it made their attentiveness metrics look better.

Of course, those changes were all logged, and with a few key strokes, we could see the history of them doing it. It didn't mislead us much. Rather than being a clever trick, it actually told us something valuable about that team's culture and level of management oversight. But it is certainly possible that being open about where we're headed will invite nefarious activity that can impact audit results. So we need to check for these things, even while we don't assume they are going to happen.

Perhaps it's to be expected that auditors classically want to reveal as little as they can about the contents of their audit, and in part to avoid those kinds of behaviors.

But there is cost to this traditionally cagey approach. While we think we avoid being misled, we give up the opportunity to be well-led. If instead we approach our audits collaboratively, we have a greater chance of being offered information instead of having to cleverly tease it out of the clients. After all, they know their operations better than we ever will, so wouldn't it be helpful to have a guide? The corollary to that is they also know how to hide stuff, likely better than we know how to find it.

Much has been written on "soft" people skills for auditors, and some audit professionals are naturals at putting clients at ease and asking questions in safe, harmless-feeling ways. But astute clients, and most of them are or they wouldn't be working for your organization, sense a mismatch in power when they have to show you all their cards, but you only show the ones you choose to. And that sense will tend to cause them to withhold cards you don't ask about.

Some readers will think this viewpoint is reckless or naïve, that to be a hard-nosed auditor, you must present an impenetrable exterior and command slavish responses. I've known many who would agree. But it's what Crucial Conversations calls a "sucker's choice" – the misperception that there are only two options – "either/or." In fact, the auditor can be collaborative, transparent, AND tough-minded. They can be independent AND have close professional relationships. They can deliver hard-hitting finding AND laugh with their clients. There's nothing in either the IIA or GAO standards that says we have to act non-collaboratively. The closest that either set of standards comes is *GAO-18-568G - Government Auditing*

Standards requires that auditors avoid situations that could lead reasonable and informed third parties to conclude that the auditors and audit organizations are not independent and thus are not capable of exercising objective and impartial judgment on all issues associated with conducting the engagement and reporting on the work. Sharing responsibility of timely and successful completion of an audit evenly with your clients and having some cake to celebrate it in a professional setting doesn't violate this standard. Independence and Mutual Purpose are not mutually exclusive.

Millennials

I've been asked whether I see auditors from the millennial generation as equally reticent to adopt a collaborative mindset. Much has been written about this group's natural inclination to work in teams and to cross-connect. Likewise, many studies suggest that millennials value harmonious work places and don't enjoy conflict.

Our experience with millennial auditors suggests that they are indeed more likely to adopt an auditing approach that involves greater degrees of collaboration. Moreover, employing a collaborative approach may be crucial to being able to attract millennials to the auditing profession. Assuming this is true, it actually argues for adopting a process like Active Auditing and using it as a recruiting tool.

At the minimum, it argues for dismantling an audit-to-client relationship that is characterized by tension or disharmony.

7 Collaborative Essentials

It is crucial to addressing the Mutual Purpose Gap, that auditors not just mask a secretive approach with terrific "people skills." They cannot just act as though they are on the same team with the clients, they must actually be on the same team. If they aren't, any client worth their salt will see right through them.

There are a few practical things that must occur to make a collaborative approach work. These include:

1. One team with clear roles
2. Joint commitment to collaborate

3.	Shared ground rules
4.	Frequent contact
5.	Vulnerable auditors
6.	Broadcast trust
7.	Mindful language

Most books about internal auditing focus on risk management, controls, fraud, and testing techniques. A core supposition of Active Auditing is that the "messy human stuff" matters and it matters almost more than the traditional canon of internal audit. Having decades of experience being tough-minded and essentially left-brained audit managers, we don't come to this lightly. Indeed, it's Lean's unrelenting focus on "respect for people" that convinced us that acknowledging the human aspects of auditing is essential.

Before we go further, we need to welcome the reader to the elephant in the room. That elephant's name is "Authority" and in most client engagements, the elephant stands on the auditor's side of the room. That's because typically in such engagements IA is in the power position. The audit is happening because we say so, and management generally can't refuse.

That means IA must speak first, loudly, and frequently that they are seeking a collaborative relationship. We have to be very good at each of the 7 Collaborative Essentials and be the first to raise our hands in *mea culpa* when we are not.

How difficult this will be has a lot to do with the existing reputation of the internal audit function. If you're known within the organization for being "turkeys" on your audits, it will be a much taller cliff to scale. However, if you have no evident reputation or a positive one, it should be much easier. Either way, it's a better place to end up and, we believe, worth the attempt. By the way, it is certainly possible that clients won't accept the offer. In such cases we fall back on a quote from Tom Peters, the extraordinarily successful management thinker and author of *In Search of Excellence* and 17 other books. He has been known to say, "you should never argue with people who disagree with you; instead, surround them with people who do."

There will be other audits and clients who will eventually see the value in an energetically collaborative approach. As you accumulate them, you can surround those who have declined your offer in the past.

Essential #1 - One Team with Clear Roles

From the beginning of the audit, starting during the preliminary discussion phase, it is crucial to think, and later behave, in terms of only one audit team, a Single Combined Team containing both audit and client personnel. And that team has the mutual purpose of delivering a successful and insightful audit to the customer.

It is therefore important to define the customer.

Customer

For most internal audit work, the organization's governing board (e.g., board of trustees, board of directors) is the customer. In the Active Auditing approach, all the roles described below are asked to come together as a single team to produce a product for this customer.

At its most simplistic, this realization should be enough to drive mutual purpose. After all, both management and IA work for the board. But of course, on the ground, in the trenches, with real humans; it takes more than that. Often the board is either too distant or too hands-off for this truth to bind the Single Combined Team together.

It could be argued that the C-Suite is the (or at least "a") customer. When Internal Audit doesn't report to the board and instead reports to the CEO or CFO, it may be appropriate to establish someone other than the board as the customer. When organizational positioning of Internal Audit is less than ideal, and therefore, not entirely independent, the customer becomes less clear. However, at the same time it becomes even more important that the customer be defined at the outset.

Some models of "customer service" acknowledge customers in every direction from a business unit (e.g., internal customers, external customers, and stakeholders).

In this regard, we find the view of assignment of customer under both the Agile and Lean models to be the best. In those contexts, the customer is the "entity paying for the product." Translating that to the internal audit context, the product is the audit report and the underlying assurance that goes with it – inclusive of findings and management action plans.

Single Combined Team Roles

Defining the following roles is necessary in an Active Audit, no matter how small, and we recommend they be specifically assigned at the outset.

It is with this team we are endeavoring to create mutual purpose.

- Governance Layer Owner
- Chief Audit Executive
- Business Owner
- Audit Owner
- Client Team Members
- Audit Team Members
- Audit Oversight
- Other Client Stakeholders

GOVERNANCE LAYER OWNER

The "layered" concept of governance was brought into focus by Peter Osterio, of the Osterio Group, in about 1999. He posited that in any organization there are three layers:

1. Governance Layer
2. Management Layer
3. Performance Layer

Each of these layers has a different job. The governance layer is made up of those who define organizational objectives and accept risks to those objectives. The management layer takes those objectives and finds ways to execute them. The performance layer is made up of "doers," including line supervisors, who are executing instructions from the management layer.

The governance layer is usually made up of the organization's board and its executive team. When functioning appropriately, together they define what success looks like organization-wide. They set objectives.

They also define risk tolerances, which is a very important concept. What is good enough? Are we wanting 90% on-time delivery or is 85% good enough? Do we want 2% defects, or can we accept 6%? What's the vision? These are policy choices that can only be established by the governance layer. After all, 2% defects may be prohibitively expensive relative to our customers' needs.

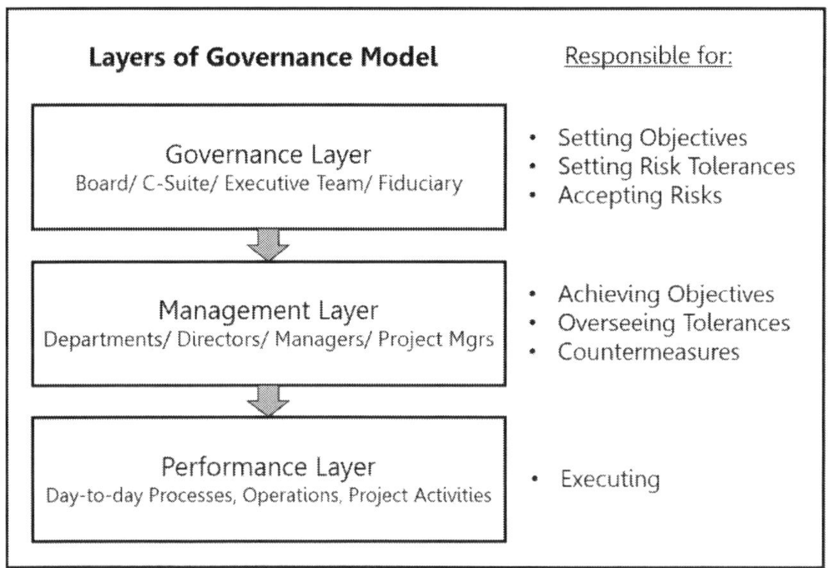

This model is different from the classic three lines of defense model, and a reasonable way to link the two models is to say that the governance model is the first line of defense expanded into its component parts.

Every audit should have a Governance Layer Owner, usually drawn from the ranks of the C-suite, though not always. In large organizations, it's possible that the governance layer extends a few layers deep into the organization. So, for an audit in Finance, it's probably the CFO. But if a direct report to the CFO has full authority to define risk tolerances and accept risks, they might be the Governance Layer Owner.

The Governance Layer Owner, also referred to as the executive owner or executive sponsor, may not be very involved in the audit, but they need to be well-informed and committed to a partnership with IA for Active Auditing to work.

In an Active Audit, the Governance Layer Owner is jointly responsible for successful completion of the audit alongside the Chief Audit Executive. In many respects, together with the Chief Audit Executive, they form the "steering committee" of the audit engagement.

I'm often asked how to get a Governance Layer Owner to accept this responsibility. The answer has multiple parts.

1. The Chief Audit Executive should discuss implementing an Active

Audit approach with their board and C-suite and ask for their explicit support. If the audit committee and CEO are committed, it's easier to convince individual Governance Layer Owners.

2. At the earliest stage of the audit, the Chief Audit Executive and the Governance Layer Owner should specifically discuss roles and jointly decide whether to "go traditional" or "go Active." It's possible they would prefer the traditional audit approach.

3. The Chief Audit Executive should openly discuss that if they jointly choose an Active Audit approach, and it isn't working, the Chief Audit Executive and Governance Layer Owner will meet and discuss countermeasures – including returning to a traditional approach.

CHIEF AUDIT EXECUTIVE ROLE

Across the aisle from the Governance Layer Owner is the Chief Audit Executive. Whether or not they are regarded as part of the executive team themselves, Chief Audit Executives have a special role to work closely with their governance layer counterpart. It's crucial that the Chief Audit Executive partner with the Governance Layer Owner to ensure mutual purpose. If this can't happen, it may not be possible to use an Active Audit approach.

When we think of the Chief Audit Executive and the Governance Layer Owner as forming the "steering committee" for the audit, the Chief Audit Executive is the Chairperson. They set the agenda and, again, because they are usually have authority on their side and are in the power position, it is the Chief Audit Executive who must extend a hand in collaboration first.

The degree to which the Chief Audit Executive and Governance Layer Owner are directly involved in any particular audit work is entirely dependent on the size and structure of the organization and the audit team. In very large and/or very regulated organizations, individual audits may be happening too frequently or too far beneath the Governance Layer Owner for the Chief Audit Executive to seek mutual purpose for each one individually. It may be most appropriate for the Chief Audit Executive and Governance Layer Owner to come together and review the annual audit plan and establish a commitment to mutual purpose around a set of audits. Then throughout the year, it would be appropriate for the Chief Audit Executive and Governance Layer Owner to connect periodically to keep lines of communication open.

As the "steering committee," the Chief Audit Executive and Governance Layer Owner are also essentially the first court of appeal if things aren't working out on the audit or if observations or findings are growing difficult to sort through. So the connection between the two needs to be established early and maintained at levels appropriate to the organization.

We recommend establishing a routine meeting schedule between the Chief Audit Executive and Governance Layer Owner during any audit. Timing depends on the situation but should be frequent enough ensure that miscommunication can't run very far before the Chief Audit Executive and Governance Layer Owner, acting together, can address it.

BUSINESS OWNER ROLE

The Business Owner is the management layer representative for the audit. Coming from the business side, they need to be sufficiently senior that they can ensure the responsiveness of the Client Team Members across the whole scope of the audit. On the other hand, the Business Owner should not be so highly placed that they can't come to Standups or other meetings or respond in timely ways.

Ideally the Business Owner comes to most Standups. When they cannot, they should arrange for information to flow to them about status and open tasks.

For large audits, perhaps with sizeable sub-areas, it's best not to allow multiple owners or owners who join or drop off after certain sections are complete. It may be unavoidable, but when this occurs, crucial continuity is often lost. If it happens, the Single Combined Team should recognize that it can be more damaging to a collaborative approach than it might appear and address it directly. Special efforts to bring new Business Owners up to speed will likely need to occur.

AUDIT OWNER ROLE

The Audit Owner role mirrors the Business Owner role.

It's important to understand the Audit Owner role in an Active Audit context and how it differs from an auditor-in-charge. While the term auditor-in-charge is common in many internal audit shops, in some cases, the term refers to a skilled auditor who has a great deal of authority and in others, their authority is significantly more limited – for example acting as the on-the-ground representative of a non-traveling audit manager who may have remained at headquarters. In such cases, they are responsible for delivery but not defining the audit work.

In an Active Audit context, the role of Audit Owner refers to the audit staff person who is principally responsible for defining the subject areas in scope for the audit and establishing the schedule of Iterations. They likely receive significant input from their supervisors and fellow auditors, but they've got primary decision-making authority to set the scope of work and create a plan to achieve it.

While the Audit Owner role is critical, it's important to remember that all normal oversight and approval processes required by professional auditing standards are still done in an Active Audit environment. Risk assessments, audit programs, workpapers, observations, and reports all receive review and approval by someone in an oversight position.

When acting in this manner, an Audit Owner takes on a role similar to an Agile Product Owner. An Agile Product Owner grooms the feature "Backlog," sets priorities, establishes release schedules, and acts as the "voice of the customer." The Audit Owner does these same things in an internal audit context.

To further the equivalence, the set of subject areas within an audit can be thought of as analogous to an Agile Product Backlog. And the risk analysis, led by the Audit Owner, is the tool for defining priorities. The priorities ultimately lead to decisions around which subject areas and Control Objectives are included in the audit's scope.

Then the Audit Owner works with the Business Owner to assign those Control Objectives to audit Iterations or Sprints. This is somewhat different from most traditional audit approaches, where the auditors primarily define what work will be done in which order – sometimes advising the clients and sometimes not.

CLIENT TEAM MEMBERS

Not surprisingly, the client team is made up of the performance layer management and staff who do the work being audited. In our experience, this is usually a cross-disciplined team, sometimes including staff from closely associated areas or, in some cases, the legal team. The client team should be defined fairly widely to include anyone the auditors think they may need to interview or interact with during the engagement.

Often in traditional audit approaches only supervisors and lead personnel are included in entrance meetings and status updates. Frequently, the rest are sent an email or briefed in a staff meeting about the audit and warned that they might be contacted.

That doesn't fly in an Active Audit.

Remember, we're attempting to blow up the model that says audits are done on a "need to know" basis. Including as many staff as possible who might find themselves encountering the audit or auditors, in addition to all those who might be affected by its findings, should be "in on it" to the extent their time and workload allows.

As part of the Single Combined Team dedicated to delivering a successful and insightful audit, the Client Team Members have a primary duty to share information, provide context and perspective, and stay current with the status of the audit work. To the extent Client Team Members can become guides and helpers, the audit work will be better, more efficiently completed, and more insightful.

AUDIT TEAM MEMBERS

This role refers to the auditors assigned to conduct field work. In small IA teams, this could be a single auditor and that auditor may also be the Audit Owner. In larger audit teams for a given audit, this team could be many auditors.

As you might expect, the Audit Team Members do most of the interviewing, testing, data analytics, documenting, and report writing for the audit. In an Active Audit, however, more than in traditional auditing, they become ambassadors. Their behavior with the clients and the ways in which they interact will mark the success or failure of the collaborative approach.

Like players on a football field, they need to hold each other accountable for how they interact with the clients, and their coaches (usually the Audit Owner and audit management) need to constantly reinforce a collaborative mindset.

AUDIT OVERSIGHT

This is the person who will be reviewing and approving the audit's components for quality, lack of bias, and completeness. Depending on staff size and organizational structure, it might be an audit supervisor, or it might be the Chief Audit Executive. Being that the term doesn't roll off the tongue, some teams might find it useful to refer to this role by title – e.g., Audit Manager or Team Lead. For IA teams structured in other ways, where oversight is provided by a senior but not supervisory employee, it also might be useful to refer to it as Quality Assurance or Quality Control. As in, "QA will be done on this audit by Sally, who is leading a different audit, but will devote the time."

Single-person IA shops find various ways to fulfill this role – sometimes using individuals from their Legal Departments or a disinterested manager in another area. In the worst case, single-person IA teams are forced to do both the Audit Owner and Audit Oversight roles.

No matter how it is accomplished, it needs to meet Standard 2340 of the *International Standards for the Professional Practice of Internal Auditing* and ensure the IA function can meet Standard 1300 (from the 2017 *International Standards*):

2340 – Engagement Supervision

Engagements must be properly supervised to ensure objectives are achieved, quality is assured, and staff is developed.

Interpretation:

The extent of supervision required will depend on the proficiency and experience of internal auditors and the complexity of the engagement. The chief audit executive has overall responsibility for supervising the engagement, whether performed by or for the internal audit activity, but may designate appropriately experienced members of the internal audit activity to perform the review. Appropriate evidence of supervision is documented and retained.

1300 – Quality Assurance and Improvement Program

The chief audit executive must develop and maintain a quality assurance and improvement program that covers all aspects of the internal audit activity.

Interpretation:

A quality assurance and improvement program is designed to enable an evaluation of the internal audit activity's conformance with the *Standards* and an evaluation of whether internal auditors apply the Code of Ethics.

The program also assesses the efficiency and effectiveness of the internal audit activity and identifies opportunities for improvement. The chief audit executive should encourage board oversight in the quality assurance and improvement program.

While it's a bit of a "tortured analogy," one could draw a parallel between the Audit Oversight role and a QA or Testing Manager in an IT setting. However, a pure Agile approach doesn't usually assign this role to a single person. Instead, Agile's self-organizing teams usually conduct testing and QA within their own ranks.

OTHER CLIENT STAKEHOLDERS

In a past organization, every time we conducted an audit of a non-financial area, we would tug on strings that would lead us back to the Finance Department. We'd start out looking at a capital project and find an issue in how fixed assets were being recorded. Or we'd be looking at Customer Service and find an issue with how cash was being transmitted to Treasury. Suddenly we'd be requesting an interview in Finance and none of those employees knew there was an audit going on. They hadn't been to any Standups and in some cases had never encountered the Internal Audit team. Yet, suddenly, we needed them to drop everything and work on our thing.

This did not help generate mutual purpose, and mitigating the disruption and anxiety would often consume IA management for hours or days.

The lesson here is to recognize this at the outset and define your set of Other Client Stakeholders and include them from the start. They may only attend one or two Standups or meetings, but they will be introduced to the auditors and the subject of the audit before they are needed. It's cheap insurance against the chance you tug a string that leads to their area.

Depending on organization structure, it may also be wise to touch base with any governance layer leaders that sit above your Other Client Stakeholders early in the audit.

Essential #2 - Joint Commitment to Collaborate

The auditors can't just take for granted that the Governance Layer Owner and Business Owner want to collaborate. It takes a specific discussion and a specific moment whereby all the members of the Single Combined Team go "all in" on choosing to collaborate.

Arriving at this moment takes a bit of behind-the-scenes work, usually done in the preliminary phase of the audit. It starts with the Chief Audit Executive and the Governance Layer Owner meeting and agreeing to support a collaborative approach. Next, the Audit Owner and Business Owner need to discuss what a collaborative approach looks like and why it can be better for all involved. It won't be possible to operate the audit collaboratively if either the Governance Layer Owner or Business Owner are unwilling to commit alongside the auditors.

And there is another potential trap waiting.

That trap is to achieve apparent commitment when there is not full understanding of what it means. This can happen when the Chief Audit Executive and/or Audit Owner don't explain the approach well or gloss over the parts that require client involvement. If either the Governance Layer Owner or Business Owner commit but are confused or misunderstand the nature of an Active Audit at the outset, it's a ticking time bomb. When it goes off, it can be deadlier to the successful completion of the audit than if you didn't attempt a collaborative approach at all. Both the auditors and the clients will feel betrayed, and betrayal is a powerful emotion.

Assuming the Governance Layer Owner and Business Owner are on-board, it's time to ask the remaining team members to commit. This is usually done at the first Standup, which typically is a bit longer than later versions – perhaps 30 or 45 minutes.

The highest-ranking member on the audit side of the team, perhaps the Audit Owner or Audit Oversight, starts by saying something like the following:

"Folks, thanks for being here. We appreciate you being a part of the audit team. It is this team's goal to deliver a successful, on-time, and insightful audit to the board. Some of you may have been involved in internal audits before and some of you may believe you know how they work. Here at XYZ Widgets, as often as we can, we run a different kind of audit process from what you may have experienced before, here or elsewhere. It's built on Lean and Agile principles, and it involves a ton of close collaboration. We think it leads to better audits, makes the work go faster, and makes everyone involved happier. We'd like to offer that approach to you for this audit. If you take us up on it, here's what to expect:

- We won't keep secrets from each other — the auditors will commit to telling you

everything they can about what they're doing. In return, we'll ask that you help lead us through your business so we can understand it properly.

- We'll all be together in a Standup frequently. That probably means every day for about 15 minutes – maybe less at the beginning and towards the end of the audit.

- Before anything is shared to the board or senior management, you'll have a chance to comment and provide perspective and additional information.

- We'll all respect that each of us here has an important job to do and we will help each other do it.

- We'll all behave as though we are one single team which has a mutual purpose.

You can choose to decline, which will be disappointing because we think a less collaborative approach doesn't work as well and leads to less happy people, but we understand if you have reservations."

It's likely that folks will have questions, which you can handle now, or you can defer. Following questions, the next person to speak should be the highest-ranking member of the client side of the team – perhaps the Governance Layer Owner or Business Owner. They don't need to say much, but in pre-conversations they should have been coached to speak up in support. Something like the following usually is sufficient:

"Team, I've talked with the auditors about this approach and it seems like it could work for us. I see the value in us acting as a single team to deliver this audit. The auditors will still be tough on us; that's their job. But I believe they are committed to working with us on the audit and I've got an open line of communication with them to be sure it works well. We're all going to be feeling our way here together and I say we give it a try."

Following a statement of support like this, it's time to ask for commitment.

I've used several techniques for gathering commitment in the past. One is to ask everyone to stand if they can commit to such an approach and remain standing if they will commit. Another is to ask everyone in the group to put up fingers to indicate their level of commitment – five fingers meaning they are "all in."

We need everyone at five to go forward.

If anyone puts up less than five, take a moment to find out why. Ask questions and see what might make them more committed. Whatever method is used, it is important to have a deliberate moment where the entire team commits to at least trying a collaborative approach.

The script for asking for commitment might go something like this:

"Well, it's time to decide how we're going run this audit. Please indicate how committed you are to trying a collaborative approach to this audit by raising some number of fingers. Five fingers mean you are all in and ready to give it a try. If you are generally liking the idea and willing to give it a try, but have some questions - maybe put up four fingers and we can discuss what you might need clarification on.

So, where is everyone now? Say, Lucy, I see you have only three fingers up. What hesitations do you have?"

Incidentally, it is okay for the Audit Owner or Chief Audit Executive to put up less than five fingers, particularly if they sense the group isn't fully aligned. Any hesitations that can be talked about now will be less likely to submarine the audit effort later when the stakes are higher.

Essential #3 - Shared Ground Rules

Ground rules are for "equals." Perhaps more directly, there is a difference between "rules" and "ground rules." "Rules" come from authority. "Ground rules" come because we all agree how we want to work together.

It is essentially impossible to run a truly collaborative Active Audit without Shared Ground Rules that are fair and honest to both sides.

Right now, some veteran auditors will be saying, "Wait a minute, the auditees don't get to choose how the audit is going to run. They don't get to negotiate with us. What if we negotiate away something important? After all, our Audit Charter says we have 'unrestricted access' to **anything** we want to see in the course of the audit. Why do we have to bend?"

Of course, that thinking is a continuation of the "sucker's choice," the idea that we can be collaborative, <u>or</u> we can be hard-nosed. Fortunately, there are more options than that, and recognizing them establishes a healthy relationship with your clients.

You are seeking "and," not "or."

The key is to outline your "non-negotiables" and recognize that your clients are likely to have some as well.

Typically, strategic-level non-negotiables for auditors are things like:

- We are obligated to follow-up on significant risks and potential issues as we find them – even if they weren't in our original scope.
- The contents and conclusions of the audit report are ultimately up to the internal auditors.
- We have unrestricted access any personnel, documents, or data that we believe are necessary to fulfill our duty.
- We are paid to be skeptical, so we will ask tough questions.
- Everyone on the Single Combined Team will attend Standups as often as they can. Non-attendance won't be an excuse for not knowing what's going on.
- The Governance Layer Owner and Chief Audit Executive will meet regularly, on a defined schedule.

We might even have more tactical non-negotiables:

- If it isn't written down, we can't accept it was done.
- We need the raw data, not a report summarizing it.
- Supervisors should not expect to attend interviews of their subordinates.

Clients should advance their own requirements, and they will; particularly when they find out you actually care what they are. Some that frequently appear are:

- When you schedule my people to meet with you, I'd like to know.
- Before anything is published to my boss or the board, I expect to see it and have an opportunity to comment.
- During X and Y weeks, my folks will be unavailable. They have a month-end activity that consumes everyone's capacity.

Most client non-negotiables aren't really difficult to agree to. If they suggest a non-negotiable you truly believe you can't accommodate for independence reasons or otherwise, you'll need to call it out – obviously with respect and humility.

Perhaps their requirement is they expect to be present for every interview of their subordinates. I've encountered this demand many times and, of course, experienced auditors know that they get different answers when the boss is in the interview room. Moreover, especially self-aware auditors accept that they ask questions differently when the boss is present.

Usually this is a requirement auditors can't accept. Better to address it in a discussion about Shared Ground Rules than later when it becomes a flashpoint.

I suspect most auditors have arrived at interviews to find others have invited themselves. This creates a tricky moment. If the auditor excuses or attempts to excuse the supervisor, the supervisor is likely to "lose face." That doesn't contribute to mutual purpose. An embarrassed supervisor will "get even." I've had it happen. On the other hand, if the auditor allows the supervisor to remain, it jeopardizes the cleanliness of the information gathered.

So it's much healthier and more respectful to discuss this when setting Shared Ground Rules.

Perhaps for some interviews you can allow the supervisor to attend. I've often found that after they attend one or two, and find the auditors are treating their people with respect, they stop coming. Perhaps you can agree to "check in" with the supervisor regarding any information that you hear that seems to be generating a potential observation. Such an offer tends to counter a form of many a client's preeminent fear, described under Pillar One, in which an auditor learns something from a subordinate and doesn't fully understand the context before writing an observation.

Client requirements exist, whether you get them out in the open or not. And clients aren't going to make them negotiable, just because you didn't ask. They will show up to interviews (or whatever it is) and compel you to excuse them if you don't agree beforehand.

I've seen some audit teams have success capturing the most common non-negotiables in a pre-printed service level agreement. However, doing so has some risk, since it can come off as authoritative and crush the feeling of authentic dialog. A laminated page of pre-typed agreements doesn't look very collaborative. Nothing wrong with drafting them together though.

We recommend taking time either in an early Standup meeting or in a separate "opening" meeting with the Governance Layer Owner and Business Owner to directly address and capture Shared Ground Rules. However, don't just jot them down and keep them in your notes. Post them where the group can see them.

Lean teaches that, when in doubt, grab tape and post a copy on your Visual Control Board.

If you are using a large whiteboard as the base of your Visual Control Board (discussed later), perhaps just mark out a section and handwrite them. Stickies also work well, as does a taped piece of blank paper. The point is they are referenceable throughout the audit and can be used to head off conflict.

Two Ways

In their book, *Leadership and Self-Deception: Getting out of the Box*, the Arbinger Institute posits that there are always two ways to interact with people – inside the box or outside of it. The "box" is a metaphor for whether a person treats another as an object or as a real person. The book suggests that all of us make this choice many times a day and when we are out-of-the-box towards someone, our relationships are much more effective. Interestingly, it is possible to be in-the-box towards one person in a group and out of it towards the person standing next to them. Humans are complicated beasts.

They use the example of firing a subordinate. If you are in-the-box towards that subordinate, your language will be distant and clinical, you won't look for ways to treat them humanely – and you won't even realize you are doing it. If you are out-of-the-box, your language will be different – more personal and caring. Even your facial expressions will communicate that even though you are still dismissing them, they are a real person to you and how they feel matters.

The book's point is that in any action (even firing someone) you can choose to do it one of the two ways. One way will likely result in the subordinate disliking you and the organization they are leaving. They'll have a "bad taste." If they meet you again, you're both likely to look at your shoes and keep the dialog to a few words. The other way gives you both a much better chance to maintain a positive relationship, even after a tough moment like a dismissal.

Viewed through this lens, our non-negotiables can be advanced two ways – one where the clients are objects and another where they are real human beings.

In our first example, "We are obligated to follow up on significant risks and potential issues as we find them – even if they weren't in our original scope," this can be done two ways.

The in-the-box way (objects) will have us stating this as a fact and crossing our arms to show we're not to be argued with.

The out-of-the-box way (real people), doesn't back down on the point, but it will likely have us promising that if this occurs, we will make every effort to inform the client immediately, certainly by the next Standup, and we commit to minimizing any disruption that results.

Energetic Collaboration requires we do our best to stay out-of-the-box with our clients.

What's the Product We're Making?

It's actually fairly easy to assemble a team and give them things to do, without answering the question, "What are we making?" or "Why are we here?" I see it in meeting etiquette all the time. An enthusiastic group comes together and begins discussion, without any clear idea of the goal of that discussion. You've probably seen it too.

It's equally easy to walk right past the goal(s) of an audit.

If you were to line up a group of young auditors engaged in a typical audit and ask them, in your best drill sergeant voice, "Son, why are you here?!," you are likely to hear a variety of partial answers.

The most likely, as the young auditor salutes and puffs out his chest, is something like, "To provide assurance to our board, Sir!" You might hear, "To help make things better!" Faced with such a question, I might quote from the templatized internal audit charter and say, "I'm here to assist the organization with the execution of its mission. I do so by evaluating whether adequate and effective risk management, governance, and internal control procedures are in place and are functioning effectively, Sir!"

These are fine textbook answers, but they don't really address the question from the client's perspective. The client wants to understand the power dynamic in the situation. They want to know how much of what the auditors are about to say, they are required to do. They want to understand what's negotiable, the boundaries of that negotiation, and where their authority lies to continue to set the direction for their business.

I have a sneaking suspicion that we auditors ignore the "product question" semi-intentionally. If we can leave the goal undefined, we remain in control. The clients remain on their "back foot." The goal is whatever we say it is. After all, "We're the ones asking the questions here."

In an Active Audit, there is a better way; one that is consistent with Pillar One.

In my experience, there are five products of a typical "assurance" engagement. In any single audit, you may produce all five. They are delimited based on the role the client is obligated to play.

In an Active Audit the key is to acknowledge they are different and to treat them differently. If the differences are ignored in how you communicate and how you place them in the audit report, the client gains an affirmative right to react negatively. The first two types are easy to handle, the following three are less so.

The most common product types are:

Type One – Affirmation: Affirmation is confirming to management and the board that things are working mostly as expected. Audits that result in 100% affirmation won't have any published findings. Of course, every client is hoping this will be the sole product of their audit. Auditors should be equally happy delivering affirmation as they are any of the other types. If the facts say things are in good order, the auditors have done "work worth paying for" to tell that story.

Type Two – Fix already in Process: One step up from affirmation is confirming to management and the board that there is an issue, but efforts were already underway to mitigate it before commencement of the audit. The client doesn't need to do anything except stay the course. Some auditors get confused whether this product type should be reported. Mostly, the answer is yes, because the risk usually still exists until the mitigation action is complete. If the day after the auditors publish the report, the project to fix the issue gets cancelled, we'll have given an incorrect impression of the control situation if the report didn't emphasize the need to carry out the planned mitigation. Likewise, you short change your client by failing to mention areas where the client already understood the risks and had initiated action.

Type Three – Fix can occur immediately: Often a finding is simple enough that it can be fixed before the audit is complete. Clients often ask whether such things need to be reported. From the client's point of view, this question strikes at the heart of the auditor's motivations and says a lot about whether there really is mutual purpose. Report every "quick fix" finding and you can be reasonably accused of "counting coup" or "trophy hunting." The report becomes an inventory of how successful the auditors were at discovering issues, not a tool for continuous improvement. Reporting even a summary of quick fixes can look like the auditors are trying to paint a certain picture of the quality of management in the area and this painting can be light or dark depending on the colors used. It could read, "Hey look at these guys; they had loads of issues they could have fixed themselves, but they weren't paying attention. They're schmucks!" Or, it could portray how attentive management was to the auditors. Unfortunately, even the latter can appear self-serving. It says, "Look at how they did what we told them. See how influential we auditors are."

So, be extra attentive to how you are portraying issues and use organizational risk as your guide. Report high risks and set aside lower risks in this product type.

Type Four – Fixes are Complicated: Most audit findings that are truly insightful fall into this type. Except in weak control environments, most of the easy-to-fix stuff should have been handled by the first or second lines of defense. The interesting findings are those that management had a difficult time seeing for themselves. These are the findings worth allowing management to consider deeply. Management will need time to figure out the right solution.

Lean tells us that proper solutions should begin as experiments before being uniformly adopted. It also tells us that the people doing the work need to arrive at the solution. This means pushing for instant answers is inappropriate. It serves the auditor's interests, not the organization's.

We'll discuss how Active Auditing handles observations, findings, and mitigating action plans more in Pillar Two. However, at this point in terms of establishing an honest and respectful relationship between the auditors and clients, it's important to recognize that there are at least two sub-types of Type Four:

1. Findings related to better efficiency
2. Findings related to risk reduction

I can say honestly that I have confused these two sub-types many times in my career. Obviously, they are related, but when you ask a client to decide what they want to do about an observation or finding, without delineating the sub-type, you confuse them.

There is an ominous feel to "accepting the risk" of a finding related to risk reduction, whereas deciding to ignore an opportunity presented by the auditors for better efficiency feels more like them making rational business decisions. Yet, in reality, they are both just business decisions.

Type Five – Suggestions: Many observations are just good ideas. The auditors see a way they think will make things better. Perhaps we are quoting "best practice" discovered during our initial research. That best practice was probably built into the audit program and Control Objectives. The observation might even have come directly from one of the IIA's guides for auditing subject areas. This is good stuff, and the clients should listen, right?

Maybe, probably.

However, when we auditors present Type Five products as though they are Type Three or Four, we commit an unforgivable sin and we will go straight to auditor purgatory when we die. On the other hand, when we honestly portray them for what they are, we do the organization a real service. And if we don't purposefully declare which is which, our clients will assume we think they are Type Fours, and this will erode our sense of mutual purpose.

Every audit will have a mix of the above. When establishing Shared Ground Rules, we recommend having a deliberate discussion with the Business Owner and Governance Layer Owner about the differences in product types. Be open and promise that you will do your best to not confuse the types during the audit. Also, offer to accept the feedback fairly if you do. It's not always easy to notice, while you are in the middle of the work, whether an issue is just best practice or a real risk.

It's also important to avoid confusing our products with our purpose. Beyond any single type of product IA produces, there is a reasonable argument that merely having someone watching management exerts positive influence and changes how the organization behaves.

Essential #4 – Frequent Contact

"Out of sight, out of mind." To build Energetic Collaboration, it is necessary for the Single Combined Team to be with each other frequently, acting with mutual purpose.

I've mentioned Standups several times. In Active Auditing, Standups are the chief way in which auditors and clients maintain frequent contact.

Standups are a technique used both in Lean and Agile environments. They are short, structured get-togethers designed to ensure everyone is on the same page, assign tasks, and celebrate successes.

Indeed, the term Scrum, which is one form of Agile development, derives from this technique and is borne from the sport rugby. In rugby, when the game continues following an infraction, up to eight players from each team interlock arms and the ball is fed into the middle of the mass. It's the classic rugby image, 16 athletes all hugging each other on the field of play. Evidently, the early founders of Agile Scrum saw similarity between the tight huddle of players fighting to take possession of the ball, and software developers hashing out code.

Standups are typically no more than 30 minutes, with 15-20 minutes being common. We found the following to be key elements of an effective Active Audit Standup:

- Hold them at least two times a week, Monday and Thursday at a minimum.
- Hold them as often as every day during the meat of the audit work.
- Hold them at the same time each day in the same place.
- All members of the client team attend as much as they can. If they can't attend, they enlist a coworker to brief them afterwards.
- Attendance is taken and posted.
- The same pattern of discussion is followed each time.
- The Standup can be led by any member of the Single Combined Team. Indeed, all members of the team are encouraged to lead from time to time.
- Standup takes place even if large parts of the Single Combined Team aren't present.
- When the Iteration schedule is known, those team members not included in the current Iteration can choose to come less

frequently, but not stop altogether.

- Continue holding Standups until the audit report is issued.

There are entire books written on keeping Standups or "Scrums" interesting for participants. We recommend referencing a few and Googling the subject if your Standups become tired or dull.

For now, the most crucial technique we offer is to regularly have food (and not just sweets) available. Standups set for 2:00, with a mix of things that are good and good for you are pure gold in your quest for a collaborative audit. Folks will find ways to attend. After all, neighborliness has been defined for centuries by folks bringing by homemade cookies, fudge, or (in my younger days) zucchini bread to the farmhouse down the road.

Beyond Standups, we recommend personal contact over, or in addition to, email and phone, whenever possible. A previous boss of mine would often say, "I've looked around my office, and the control environment looks pretty good in here - maybe I should go see how it is elsewhere!" Get out of your office (or your assigned conference room) and meet with people.

Frequent contact is not constant contact, however. Make it scheduled, make it short, and allow for the opportunity to laugh about something other than the data you are requesting or the interview you are conducting. Let the clients retreat to their spaces afterwards.

Much of the content of the Standup is driven by / aided by the Visual Control Board. So we'll discuss more about what specific work gets done during a typical Standup in Pillar Three – Visual Management. You've already got a sense of it, because you experienced a Standup in the opening story.

Essential #5 - Vulnerable Auditors

At the first Standup of the first Active Audit we ever tried, I explained the methodology we intended and mentioned that it was unusual. I explained that my team and I believed it was better for everyone.

The clients did not seem convinced, and several of them looked like they might be thinking we were trying to "con" them.

In that moment, I realized I'd need to do something authentic to let them know we were serious. Even so, I was a little scared to "bare my soul."

Our Standup leader, the Audit Owner, was "going around the room" and asking if anyone had further comments or questions. The responses confirmed my concern that the clients weren't willing to trust a different approach.

So, I lurched a bit and said, "Yeah, I do. I need to say something."

My face got serious (and probably a bit red) and I said, "You know, I believe in this approach, I think it's the right thing to do, and logically it makes perfect sense. But, I gotta tell ya, it doesn't come naturally to me. I've got a lot of years doing audits the normal way and I don't know where or how this is gonna go. I'm totally out of my comfort zone and I just want everyone to know that. So, if you see me struggling or I say the wrong thing, it's not because I don't believe in doing things this way… I've just got a lot more experience doing it the other way. I've got habits I'll personally need to break."

It took the group a bit by surprise, if for no other reason than a Chief Auditor carries around a scary almost inhuman reputation and folks weren't accustomed to seeing me unguarded.

We had, on that team, a terrific veteran auditor who was with us on a co-source arrangement. She had more internal audit experience than I and had held chief audit executive roles in three different organizations. She was now doing consulting work. What she said in response both drove the point home and lightened the mood.

She retorted, "Yeah, it's killing me." Everyone chuckled, but also saw the honesty we were sharing.

From that exchange, our clients saw that auditors could be both vulnerable and real. And they could tell we were serious.

Because auditors are almost always in a power position over their clients, to truly become collaborative, the clients need to see the auditors become vulnerable. It levels the playing field and helps drive mutual purpose.

How you do that is as personal as your fingerprint, but it's necessary. And it's necessary that the auditors do it first.

Essential #6 - Broadcast Trust

Internal auditors are often very good readers of body language and pay close attention to specific language usage. Many of us have received training in non-verbal cues, particularly as they relate to investigations. However, fewer of us have received training in being aware of our own non-verbals, which is a critical mistake because auditors are being watched constantly.

Like parents are watched by their children who are quick to pick up on micro-expressions and code language that telegraph when a parent may be displeased, so too clients pay far more attention to the auditors than we imagine. I know this because I've asked them.

I also know this because of my training and years of experience in group facilitation. A trained facilitator can change the direction of a group by changing the way they invite responses from the participants. I confess. I am guilty of controlling the direction of focus groups and policy-making workshops. I've done it intentionally and haphazardly.

Humans in groups watch intently to understand the inherent rules of the discussion. If a facilitator uses an adjective to rephrase something a participant says, that adjective can reframe the discussion – potentially closing off an entire line of thinking.

The facilitator can also accomplish this by how they position their body. For example, if a participant is offering input the facilitator doesn't like, the facilitator can, perhaps by turning their shoulder slightly to that participant tell the group, "That line of thinking is unwelcome." A skilled facilitator can manipulate a group in this way without the participants being aware. Moreover, a sloppy facilitator can do this by accident, ruining the validity of the discussion without knowing they've done so.

The cost of this sloppy behavior in a focus group is erroneous data and the loss of time and resources related to the wasted effort. When an auditor is unaware of their non-verbal effect, they put at risk the collaborative approach to the audit. They may even damage future audits, since word invariably "gets around."

So, what does it mean to broadcast trust?

We'd start by acknowledging that most of us are far worse poker players than we may wish to believe. How we internally regard a client we are interviewing is likely to be written all over our faces and will be evident in how we ask questions. It can even extend to how we describe the audit. If we call the engagement an examination, that will generate a different subtle reaction than using the term "review" or "health check."

There are loads of books and articles written on body language and broadcasting trust. Many of them have to do with how to get people to trust you, which is very important to an auditor. However, at the moment, we are chiefly interested in making it clear that *you* trust the clients. Remember, they're studying you to see how you think of them.

Do you think they are good at their jobs? Do you regard them as objects to be studied? Do you respect them enough to listen? Will you give them a "fair shake?"

The traditional, dispassionate approach to auditing concerns itself not at all with these questions. Worse, we sometimes lapse into purposefully, and somewhat lazily, treating the clients like they are under investigation. Right now, you are saying, "I never do that." In a moment, if you're honest, you'll think of at least one time when you indeed "did that."

To broadcast trust you could start with saying something like, "You know all of this much better than I do, can you help me understand?" You could also just say, "By the way, I trust all of this is in order, I just need to be able to demonstrate that."

It can't hurt.

However, the work of psychologist Albert Mehrabian on non-verbal communication is regularly cited as proof that what you say is only 7% of the message, while 38% is intonation and 55% is body language. And while this "7-38-55" rule is often applied in conditions not directly supported by Dr. Mehrabian's original experiments, it's hard to argue that how you deliver the message is hugely important to how it is heard.

Consequently, to achieve Energetic Collaboration, becoming aware of our non-verbal behaviors is critical.

Taking many available resources in non-verbal indicators of trust together, we offer the following techniques:

- Demonstrate active listening
- Mirror their posture
- Avoid power gestures
- Demonstrate humility
- Be respectful of their time and circumstances

Demonstrate Active Listening – There are many models for active listening. We find the simple formula advised by the U.S. Department of State in coaching diplomacy to be as good as any. They advise diplomats to:

1. Seek to understand before you seek to be understood
2. Be non-judgmental

3.   Give your undivided attention to the speaker

4.   Use silence effectively and avoid interruptions

Mirror Their Posture – You may have noticed that in effective conversations, ones that go well, you wind up assuming the same position as the person across from you. If they are sitting back with their legs crossed, you will too. If they are leaned forward, you match them. This isn't coincidence. And you'll just as often find that when a conversation isn't going well, you won't be mirroring.

Humans, being tribal creatures, are regularly searching for cues that others are on the same page. Mirroring is a subtle indicator that you are on the same team.

Avoid Power Gestures – A quick indicator to your clients that you are "talking" collaboration, but really "meaning" you are in charge is the use of common power gestures. Power gestures are body language designed to demonstrate dominance. The classic power gesture is "steepling" like an evil Bond villain. This gesture is so well known by now that I've only encountered it in real life a handful of times. It's too big a "tell" for most powerful people to use to project dominance. However, there are plenty of others.

The "basketball steeple" is a gesture many politicians use, including former President Barack Obama, to establish they are in charge. It's like the classic finger steeple, except the hands are further apart, about the distance needed to hold a basketball.

Leaning back and putting your arms over your head demonstrates that you own the room. Turning your shoulder to another person indicates you don't feel you have to give them your full attention. Even simpler, crossing your arms in front of you can be read as you are projecting intensity and daring the other people in the room to match it.

There are many more and some undoubtedly which are particular to your organization. The point is to be aware of these gestures and what they may be saying to your clients. Because I haven't studied them all, I just try to use body language I'd be comfortable using if the CEO or audit committee chairperson were in the room.

Demonstrate Humility – I find that just keeping the word "humility" in my mind when interacting with clients helps change the way I project outwardly. Of course, the kind of humility to which I refer is the self-respectful kind that recognizes I don't have all the answers and I come to the interaction with, as the Zen Master Ryutan is believed to have said in the 9th century, an "empty cup."

Be Respectful of Their Time & Circumstances – Nothing demonstrates power like forcing another person to be physically present. You really are in charge if you can coerce someone to be somewhere they'd rather not be. That's what auditors do when they arrive late or allow their interviews to run long. Always start on time and always finish on time.

Essential #7 - Mindful Language

I can remember the day I broke a bad habit. Like most bad habits, I didn't even realize I was doing it. I only became aware of it when I was coaching a staff member to mind their own language with our clients.

You see, I'd gone off to some training in which active listening skills were taught. One of the techniques described was to "show that you are listening" by responding either verbally or physically. They taught us to nod or smile and to encourage the speaker to continue with small verbal comments like, "yes" and "uh-huh." Seemed like pretty good advice.

However, my version of a small verbal comment was a problem, which I didn't even realize. I'd ask a question and, as the interviewee would respond, I'd nod, make a note, and say, "Gotcha."

Of course, I meant "I get it," "I understand what you're saying."

As I was coaching a team member to avoid certain language, which I'd noticed them using, it dawned on me the number of times in an interview I would repeat the word gotcha. And then I reflected on the number of times I would say to clients, "We're not 'gotcha' auditors, we're not here to catch you doing something. We're your business partners."

What a disconnect!

I expect that most interviewees never made a conscious connection between the two. I certainly never had anyone call me on it.

However, about mid-way through my auditing career I took a side trip into brand marketing consulting. It was an opportunity to work with friends, to do something new, and it used a lot of the same analytical and strategic skills I'd used successfully in internal auditing.

Brand marketing relies on constant repetition of central concepts in ways that are fresh and attention-getting. The easiest example I would use with new clients and with marketing teams around the country was Volvo. Our clients were exclusively colleges and universities, and I'd regularly speak to groups of faculty, staff, and students about developing their institution's brand.

As I was explaining the notion of brand, I would ask the simple question, "When you think of Volvo, what's the first thought that comes to mind?" Across the U.S. and Canada, roughly 90% of the time, they would parrot back, "Safety." Which is, of course, exactly what the marketing folks at Volvo want them to say. The other 10% of responses would usually be "boxy cars" or "yuppies," but the high response rate of "safety" was essentially universal.

When I'd expand that question to BMW, the responses were a little less crisp, but still all in the same grouping. "High performance," "the ultimate driving machine," or something similar would make up about 80% of the replies. Most of the audience in these sessions wasn't made up of "high earners." Faculty and college administrators are not BMW's primary target market. But the question still instantly brought to mind the same essential idea.

Years later, I was chatting with a CEO (who is completely BMW's target market) about self-driving cars and I asked him if his BMW could self-park. He responded with great pride that a BMW is meant to be driven, it shouldn't have any such features. He had bought into BMW's brand entirely.

The point is that messaging matters and it does so subtly. You don't see Volvo running ads that say explicitly, "Our cars are safe." But the language they use, over and over again, drifts into our consciousness. Its repetition sticks with us.

So, while no one ever pointed out my frequent use of the word 'gotcha', it was out there acting against the message I was trying to convey, which was one of partnership. I can't say I was immediately able to eradicate the word from my vocabulary, but I drastically shrunk its use in favor of "I understand" or "that makes sense."

Because, in order to Energetically Collaborate, auditors must overcome years of stereotyping that paint us as stormtroopers and not partners, we can't afford many slips of the tongue, like the word gotcha.

So keep a leash on your word choices. Avoid the vernacular of investigations or police work.

I'm afraid I use the phrase "audit evidence" a lot. It was taught to me very early in my career and it's hard to drop. The problem is that it conjures in my audience's mind the idea that somewhere in the Internal Audit "police department" we have an "evidence locker," where all that audit evidence is kept, right next to the murder weapons and the drugs. Indeed, if you think of the synonyms for the word evidence, they're all police and legal terms – testimony, proof, clue, witness.

It would be like BMW using words synonymous with "low price." Such words are "off brand." They compete with the central message BMW means to convey. In our case, language that feels like it was taken from cop shows like CSI and Dragnet works against our intent to achieve mutual purpose with our clients.

It doesn't mean I can't use the term, but I need to be aware that it can act as a negative building block for the impression I'm leaving. Instead, it's probably better to just avoid characterizing information the clients provide altogether and just call it what it is – reports, procedural documentation, datasets, or whatever.

I suspect one of the reasons I find it difficult to banish the term audit evidence from my vocabulary is it is so useful and common when reviewing audit workpapers.

Ensuring that all audit procedures are supported by "sufficient appropriate audit evidence to provide a reasonable basis for his or her opinion" is taken directly from the Public Company Accounting Oversight Board's (PCAOB) Auditing Standard No. 15, the title of which is – you guessed it – Audit Evidence. The Standard goes on to describe in significant detail the meaning of the term – using words like appropriateness, relevance, and reliability.

However, to continue to torture my branding analogy, talking with clients about the term audit evidence is like Volvo talking about how fast its cars go. Volvo doesn't make slow cars. There are plenty of Volvos on the German Autobahn, where speeds are commonly in excess of 100 mph. But they don't talk about their speed, because it doesn't advance their messaging about safety. In exactly the same way, BMW doesn't make unsafe cars, but they don't make safety a primary message.

And, before we leave this subject, just a word about written observations and reports. Minding our language extends to the written word more centrally than our verbal usage. Even when they are marked "draft," written communications feel permanent to the client. When we use police language, I sometimes call it "perpetrator language," in reports or observation sheets, we put at risk the Energetic Collaboration we are seeking.

Some typical perpetrator words or phrases I've (hopefully) edited out of documents over the years include:

- The information was corroborated by…
- The manager alleged XYZ to be true...
- The manager claimed she witnessed the report being reviewed…
- We investigated…

One subtly damaging version of perpetrator language is taking credit for discovering information, when in fact the clients provided it to the auditors in good faith. This is a sure-fire way to increase the Mutual Purpose Gap.

THREE

"Failure is simply the opportunity to
begin again, this time more intelligently."
– Henry Ford

PILLAR TWO: **ITERATIVE AUDIT EXECUTION**

The most significant concept Active Auditing takes from Agile is the idea of iterative development. Iterative development is intentionally breaking the work into "time-boxed" chunks, and at the end of each chunk having a useable result. In a software development environment, that means tested code that is ready to go into production.

In an audit environment, that means having observations in the client's hands and the supporting workpapers completed and reviewed, before moving on to the next Iteration. Depending on the maturity level of your environment and your clients, it might mean having fully agreed responses to observations. Some take longer than others to figure out how to fix things.

In Agile terminology, each time-boxed Iteration is usually called a Sprint. In an Agile model, a large software development project is usually broken into many Sprints. Each Sprint contains mini versions of a normal software project.

1.   Requirements Gathering
2.   System Design
3.   Development
4.   Testing
5.   Deployment

In an Agile environment, the common step known as Requirements Gathering, or finding out what the software needs to do, takes place both at the beginning of the effort and throughout. Unlike normal or Waterfall development, requirements will come and go through the life of the project, in response to the emerging needs of the customer. They're added to a running list known as the Backlog and "groomed" by the Product Owner on a frequent basis until they are either discarded or assigned to a Sprint to be completed.

Though there is no real standard, most guides on Agile advise that each Sprint should last between two and three weeks, and work assigned to each Sprint should be matched to that timeframe. Within those weeks, software engineers will firm up requirements, design a solution, develop workable code, test it, and make it ready for movement into a live production environment – essentially ready for sale.

The Advantages of Agile

Agile aficionados usually make three big cases for why iterative development is better than its predecessor, Waterfall development. The first is the compounding advantage of small monetizable deliverables, versus one big deliverable at the end. They point out that if a typical software project takes two years, a project that delivers small pieces of software, which can be sold perhaps every six weeks, will generate more money in the same amount of time than waiting for one big finale. It works like compound interest.

The second is the frequency with which user requirements change. So, a project scoped two years in the past is fairly likely, even if it delivers on time and on budget, to no longer be exactly what is needed on the day it is delivered.

The third is general risk. Small experiments are less risky in all sorts of ways than large big-stakes projects. For one, the market may move on while the project is under development and if there is no useable product to share, management may not find out until it's too late and a lot of money has been spent.

Iteration-Based Auditing

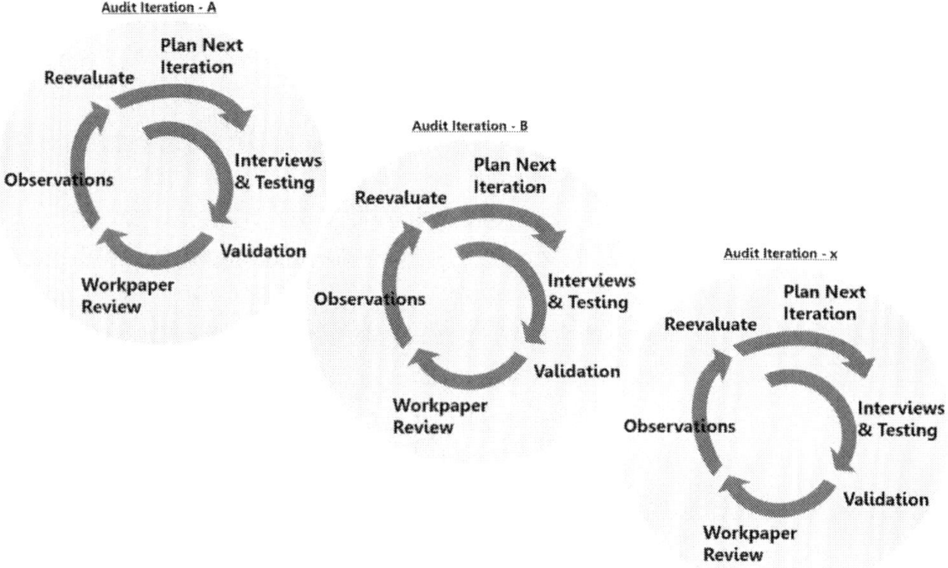

It's possible to apply these advantages to auditing, if you squint a bit. Internal auditing isn't directly about monetizing a product, and usually we view quality and depth as greater virtues than speed and time to market. Nevertheless, executing an audit in time-boxed pieces makes managing it easier in a number of ways.

An iterative audit provides the following advantages. We can…

- Take a large complex engagement and think about it in more digestible pieces.
- Tell clients when they are likely to be needed.
- View the quantity and quality of work contribution by each auditor more easily – and, if necessary, take steps to improve it while there

is still time to affect the overall audit schedule.

- Evaluate the control environment after each Iteration and decide if the depth of the fieldwork is gauged properly.
- Decide whether our original risk assessment was on-point and whether it needs to be adjusted before the next Iteration.
- Change course mid-audit based on information learned.
- Practice delivery of audit results (e.g., observations and data) with the client and start earlier to build a positive working relationship.
- Stop the audit in favor of a new priority and still have useable results.

Waterfall

It probably bears mentioning that, while proponents of Agile generally look down on Waterfall as a project management approach, far more projects get done on the planet using it than get done agilely.

Having been the Chief Internal Auditor for a major water utility that routinely devoted one-third of its very large budget to capital projects, the Waterfall approach to construction project management became second nature. An enormous number of our over 125 engineering staff either had, or were seeking, a Project Management Professional (PMP) certification which is bestowed by the Project Management Institute (PMI) and which is fundamentally based on Waterfall principles. When building a dam or constructing a pipeline, the Waterfall approach is the right tool for the job.

It is also, in my experience, the most common approach for running internal audits.

Waterfall is sequential. You gather requirements, you design the project, and you execute that project. You don't do them in a different order, and you don't reevaluate mid-stream.

Waterfall (hard-hat wearing engineers don't call it that) is common in construction because it tends to deliver predictability and certainty. Assuming the gathered requirements are very good and user changes are kept to a minimum, it becomes possible to gain certainty around the delivery outcome, timing, and cost.

Making modifications to a million yards of poured concrete after it's set is colossally expensive, if it can be done at all. And in an industry where design costs are cheap compared to materials costs and unmitigated risks can kill, certainty is highly valued.

Waterfall Development

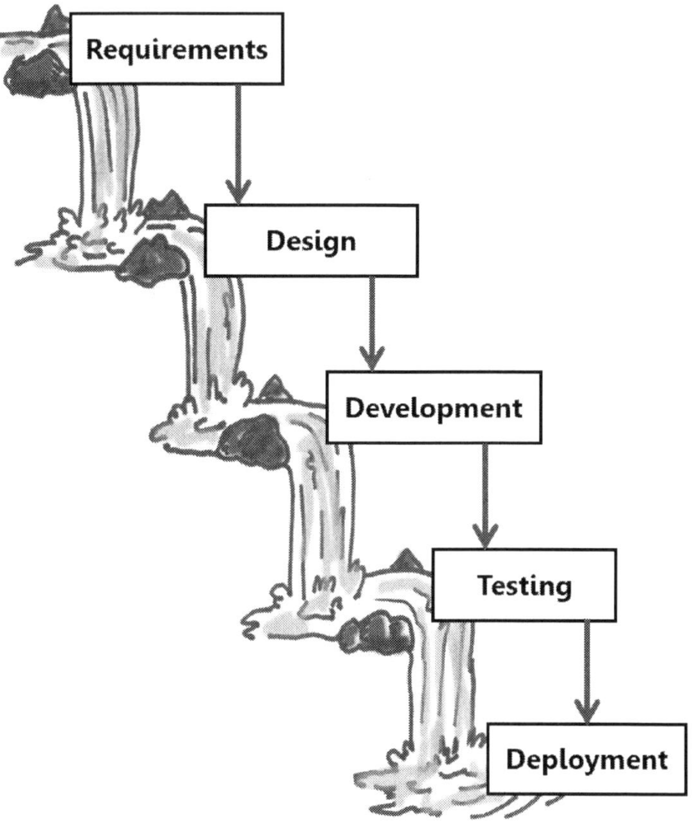

To illustrate, the engineering designs for a dam require intense amounts of scrutiny, including state and federal oversight and panels of third-party engineers to peer review the original engineer's conclusions. The consequences of bad design or poor execution are just too great. And once the design is set, the effort and costs to perform the construction are so enormous that unanticipated modifications, no matter how useful or clever, can't be allowed.

Of course, the weaknesses of Waterfall are centered in the requirements gathering and design phases, whether it is being used to develop software or to build a dam. If requirements gathering is weak or the design approach is poorly done, the potential benefit is lost. Cost and timing stop being predictable. And that predictability is arguably the whole reason to use the Waterfall approach.

IT systems are another matter. They are typified by their fluidity and, because they are usually designed to solve human business challenges, they are inherently changeable.

So too are internal audits.

Steps in a Typical Audit

While a huge proportion of internal auditors align themselves to either the Red Book (Institute of Internal Auditors – the IIA) or Yellow Book (Governmental Accounting Office – GAO), I've seldom seen any two internal audit departments run identical audit processes. Indeed, the IIA's *International Standards for the Professional Practice of Internal Auditing* understand this and are written to provide top-line guidance, while not prescribing specific business processes for auditors.

They describe <u>what</u> needs to occur, not <u>how</u>.

Fortunately, while meeting the requirements under professional standards, Active Auditing doesn't demand any particular audit process. The Pillars can be used for assurance or consulting audits, audits of any size and complexity, and audits of any length. Larger audits will likely involve more Iterations than smaller ones, but the thinking is the same. Indeed, just as with Agile, there is no requirement that there be more than one Iteration in an audit if the subject area is small.

According to *Internal Auditing: Risk & Advisory Services*, a textbook sponsored by the IIA Research Foundation, the assurance engagement process has three main steps with a collection of activities beneath each. The main steps are Plan, Perform, and Communicate.

PLAN → PERFORM → COMMUNICATE

Under 'Plan' are found steps having to do with engagement objectives and scope, understanding the auditee, assessing risk, creating a test plan and work program, and allocating resources to the engagement.

The 'Perform' step includes conducting tests, evaluating evidence to reach conclusions, and developing observations and recommendations.

The 'Communicate' step involves preliminary communications, final engagement communications, and monitoring and follow-up procedures.

In my experience, most audit teams use a rough approximation of these steps, though the exact order and how they are executed and documented are as unique to each audit department as Sunday services in two churches of the same denomination.

Most audit teams begin with a planning phase, progress to performing or conducting the audit, and finish with communicating the results. Each step follows and builds on the other, sequentially.

For those schooled in Lean and Agile, the first thing that stands out about this process is how "Waterfall-esque" it is. It relies on linear thinking, and, as such, does not deliver some of the key advantages of an iterative approach.

Like most Waterfall projects, it assumes that the planning phase will occur effectively the first time and that the resulting objectives, scope, and risk assessment will be of high quality – and will remain exactly what is needed through the life of the audit. This is a big expectation.

The textbook planning phase is analogous to the typical requirements gathering and system design phases of a Waterfall-based IT project.

It was the realization that normal requirements gathering is a profoundly flawed process that caused those rebellious founders of Agile to break with their Waterfall colleagues in the first place. In the assurance engagement process model, placing the step "understand the auditee" only at the beginning of the audit sounds logical and efficient, but ignores that true understanding takes time, direct contact, and immersion; and that as understanding grows, the next audit fieldwork to be done will likely need to change.

I suspect the classic Waterfall approach to internal auditing emerged as the dominant form for the same reason it originally occurred in IT and construction. It promises predictability. Our auditor ancestors thrived on predictability and enjoyed a much different pace of change. Moreover, predictability is a natural fit with traditional concepts of control and governance. It also seems likely that since much internal audit work in the early days of our profession was "ticking and tying" of facts and data that had already happened, there probably didn't seem to be much need for a more fluid and dynamic approach. In an environment where an internal audit function repeatedly conducts many of the same engagements, such as in compliance work, it's easier to appreciate a Waterfall approach.

Active Auditing, on the other hand, was developed in an environment where over a 10-year period, we never conducted the same audit twice. Every engagement was individually scoped and risk assessed. We needed a methodology that served us better.

And if we believe whitepapers like PricewaterhouseCoopers's *2018 State of Internal Audit* or Deloitte's *Global Chief Audit Executive Survey 2018*, the drum beat for internal auditing is calling for the same kind of flexibility and innovation that drove software development to find a different way.

Luckily, it isn't hard to modify this classic approach to be Lean and Agile.

Shifting to Active Auditing

Most of the components from the textbook assurance engagement process persist in an Active Audit, they are just done in smaller chunks and not all at once.

Essentially, if you have an audit process you like, you can keep using it. Here is how we modify it to be iterative. Keeping these principles in mind, below is a standard process for an Active Audit. Feel free to adopt as much of it as you find useful.

From Agile we take the idea of planning the engagement in broad strokes, then doing specific planning for each chunk or Iteration as the audit progresses, rather than all at once at the beginning of the audit. This allows you to build on the knowledge and understanding you gain in each Iteration. It also allows you to treat your risk assessment as flexible and adjust and change.

From Lean we take the humble realization of how little we know at the beginning of an audit. And we add to that the Lean truth that our clients often know far less than we expect about how their business is really done. That may sound crazy. But having participated in loads of Lean current state mapping exercises, it is rare for those involved in a business process to each have the same understanding of how that process works.

Active Audit Process

PRELIM.

1. Preliminary Discussion w/ Gov. Layer Owner & Bus. Owner
2. Initial Schedule

PLANNING

3. Opening Standup
4. Initial Research – SOPs, Guides, Best Practices, Etc.
5. Mini-Current State Workshops, Walkthroughs, & Gemba
6. Risk Assessment – Define most important risks with Client
7. Draft Control Objectives – Verify with Client
8. Build the Draft Audit Program – Discuss with Client
9. Iteration Planning

FIELDWORK

10. Iteration A
   - a) Interviews & Testing
   - b) Validation with Client
   - c) Workpaper Review
   - d) Workpaper Approval
   - e) Observations
   - f) Reevaluate
   - g) Plan Next Iteration

Iteration B
   - a) Interviews & Testing
   - b) Validation with Client
   - c) Workpaper Review
   - d) Workpaper Approval
   - e) Observations
   - f) Reevaluate
   - g) Plan Next Iteration

Iteration x
   - a) Interviews & Testing
   - b) Validation with Client
   - c) Workpaper Review
   - d) Workpaper Approval
   - e) Observations
   - f) Reevaluate
   - g) Plan Next Iteration

REPORTING

11. Obtain Final Agreed Actions
12. Write Draft Report – Share With Client
13. Publish Final Report

FOLLOWUP

14. Track Action Plans
15. Celebration & Retrospective
16. Close Mitigating Action Plans

When they are asked to lay out (usually using mountains of sticky notes) how their work occurs, there are invariably arguments about who has it correct. If the clients don't understand their own processes the same way, it's a trap for auditors to behave as though they can understand them properly (e.g., based on walkthrough meetings) before diving in.

PHASE - Preliminary

Not surprisingly, we begin an Active Audit using the first of the three central pillars. We seek to Energetically Collaborate. The preliminary phase is where we start that communication and set the stage for a successful audit.

1. Preliminary Discussions

It's time to sit down with the Governance Layer Owner and the Business Owner to discuss their hopes for the engagement – what would they like to see, what concerns them, where do they already know they need attention?

Whether one meeting or several, these discussions should then outline the nature of an Active Audit process, the Single Combined Team, and potential Shared Ground Rules. The discussions should finish by asking whether the Governance Layer Owner and Business Owner will support conducting the engagement using an Active Auditing approach.

Don't leave the negotiating table with any lack of understanding on the client's part about their responsibilities in an Active Audit.

Interestingly, traditional audits tend to allow clients to take a passive role. The audit is a thing being done *to* them, and they just need to answer when asked and respond to the auditor's requests. Your Governance Layer Owner and Business Owner may have played that passive role in the past and may have grown comfortable with it. Don't let them agree to an Active Audit approach with the unsaid expectation that they will sit back and let it happen to them.

2. Initial Schedule

During the preliminary phase, we have a practical but broad conversation with our clients about the timing of the audit. We need to understand reasonable boundaries for the audit. If busy season for the business unit starts in a month, we need to know that before we go any further. Likewise, we want to understand competing priorities and other challenges. If the Governance Layer Owner is expecting to be actively involved in the audit, but will be in Europe for a month, that should come to light in the preliminary phase.

Don't get too specific; we aren't planning the audit yet. We don't even know the scope.

PHASE - Planning

The key to Active Audit planning at the engagement level is to not do too much too early. Start by planning only enough to generally understand the scope and objectives so you can lay out the broad boundaries of the audit. Accept that you're going to learn a lot more as the engagement progresses.

3. Opening Standup

Again, we start with Pillar One and bring the client into the planning as early as possible. We recommend holding an initial Standup, rather than the classic "entrance meeting." The opening Standup is probably twice as long as those that follow. It is used to announce the audit and begin the dialog with the broader team. The opening Standup should occur at the Visual Control Board (discussed more later) and include as many of the Single Combined Team as possible. You'll want to cover:

- The three central pillars
- How we'll use the Visual Control Board
- Shared Ground Rules – that we'll set some now and that we'll add to them as the audit progresses
- Setting a routine Standup time and length
- Hearts & Minds discussion
- Requests for resources to begin initial research

It's not a crime if you don't get through all of these in the opening Standup; you'll be seeing a lot of each other, so just handle them as early as you can. Remember, starting and ending on time is a principle of Standups.

4. Initial Research

Depending on how much the auditors know about the subject, the first step is likely to be to conduct off-line research. There are all sorts of resources for this. The IIA publishes a number of books on how to audit common business activities. Outside books and periodicals are often available. Ask the clients what they read. Google auditing resources. It's also smart to check with your Legal Department to understand if there are laws or compliance aspects that need to be considered.

It would be tempting to try and locate someone else's audit program on the subject, and reverse engineer their fieldwork steps, but we recommend resisting that urge. Better to understand the subject and then work downward towards defining fieldwork steps. It's hard to maintain an authentic risk-based perspective if you secretly think you've got the answers to the test in your back pocket from someone else's audit.

If the audit is of something like accounts payable, or a subject you audit frequently, you may have enough basic subject knowledge in the auditor group to skip much of this research step. Don't skip it all, though. On the other hand, I've been known to send auditors to out-of-town training to gain enough basic knowledge of a complex subject to start planning. Auditors often need refreshers on subjects like construction auditing and the newest IT subject areas.

Ironically, it was this kind of preparatory research and training that brought us face-to-face with Agile for the first time.

Based on this initial research, and sticking with our human resources audit example, decide what broad chunks will be included. Will the audit focus on compensation and benefits, or will it follow the lifecycle of an employee through their time with company – perhaps beginning with recruitment and ending with offboarding? At this stage, you just want to decide the basic set of chunks. A lot of this will draw on the risk assessment work that caused your audit to appear on the annual audit plan in the first place.

Ideally, the Audit Owner makes these decisions, with input from the Audit Oversight and perhaps the Chief Audit Executive. Every organization's command structure is different, but the Audit Owner should be closest to the subject matter.

5. Mini-Planning Workshops & Gemba

Once the broad boundaries are decided, conduct a series of mini-planning workshops with your clients. Once again, we are Energetically Collaborating. Mini-planning workshops are akin to Lean current state assessments, but without the need to draw (or create with mountains of sticky notes) the detailed process diagrams.

Example: Flow Diagram

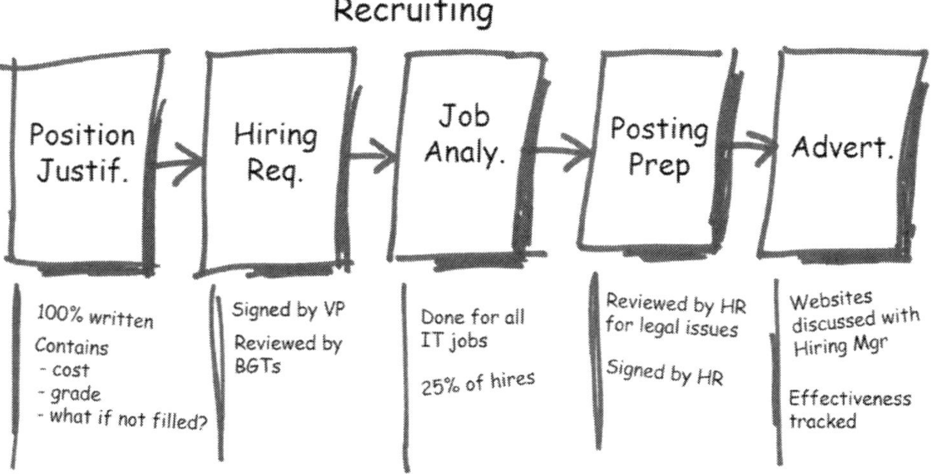

Do a mini-planning workshop with the leaders of each of the major chunks of the engagement. The objective of the workshop is to understand, from the client's point of view, what success looks like for them and what business activities must go right every day for them to achieve that success.

I find that this is best done as a "whiteboarding" exercise, a kind of structured interview using a whiteboard to capture information and play it back to the client. There are likely dozens of ways to do it. I mostly use two techniques, the choice of which depends on the variety of business processes in the chunk. If the chunk is closely contained to one important business process, then it might be appropriate to map the workflow in top-line terms, with boxes for each major sequential step.

Recruiting might be an example of this, since it usually has a clear start (the hiring manager submits some kind of requisition) and a definable end (a new employee gets hired). Flow-based boxes for recruiting might include Position Justification, Hiring Requisition, Job Analysis, Posting Preparation, Advertising, Prescreening, Interviewing, Offering & Negotiation, Background Check, Drug Screening, and Onboarding.

On the other hand, if the chunk regards benefits management, which is usually a collection of small topics, each with a fairly short business process, perhaps done by only one or two people, it might be best to draw out a component chart. You could, for example, write the title Benefits Management at the top and draw boxes underneath it that contain the key business activities.

Example: Component Chart

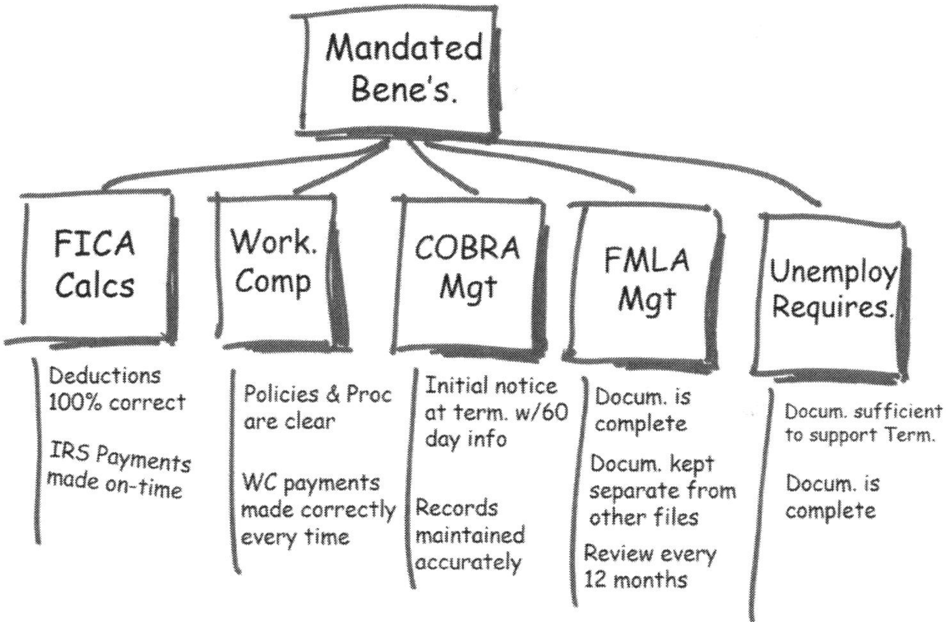

Regardless of technique, in each of these boxes you want to capture, in the client's terms, what "working properly" means, and how they know it's working properly. And most importantly, you want to do so in concert with the client. This is different from interviewing the client about their process and then drawing a diagram on Visio back at your desk. This is a shared moment of understanding. Make the most of it.

Lean often uses the phrase "what good looks like" when discussing what it means to be working properly. You want to know what success is and what represents failure. Ideally, you get these things in specific terms. If, for example, no less than 100% of all new hires must have a background check – write "100%" on the board during the workshop.

The mechanisms that management uses to know whether a process is on track are the key controls. And as any first-year auditor knows, they come in many forms. "Auditor speak" has us describing them in terms of preventive, detective, directive, corrective, etc. However, speaking like this doesn't help unlock the client's understanding of their business processes. So we've found it is better to ask the question in the client's terms – e.g., how do they know it's working, and how would they be alerted if it stopped working?

If you can get the clients to identify a specific mechanism – a report, dashboard, review and oversight cycle, or some kind of system activity that ensures things work properly – make a note on the whiteboard in the box. If they don't identify a mechanism here, it will be noticeable by its absence and the auditor can follow up with more questions later. Take a picture of the whiteboard you and the client developed together. Share it back to them.

Often, workshop participants won't know a specific target figure. It won't have occurred to them before, or they've been relying on gut feel. This alone may be an audit observation, but don't call it out as such now. Doing so ejects you out of a shared moment of understanding with the client to a position of judgment.

When the client doesn't know, ask what would be minimally acceptable. Perhaps take a poll. For example, if conducting a job analysis on a new position before it gets posted is acknowledged to be a good idea, but everyone knows it doesn't get done for every position, find out what parameters HR management uses to decide whether too few are being conducted.

The answer is probably not a single percentage. It's probably more complex than that. It will often be something like, "HR wants to be sure every new position in IT is evaluated, because the market moves quickly there. But other areas don't change much, so we do those as opportunity arises." Or, "Anything over a Grade 5 needs a review because that's where you'll see bigger salaries."

You'll need this information later to form the basis of your Control

Objectives, so it's useful to get as much of it now as possible.

Don't let each workshop dive too deeply. You just need to understand the business at a top-line level. You need enough understanding to roughly lay out the major Iterations of the audit and to start on a set of Control Objectives.

Relax and recognize the limitations of a single-pass information gathering workshop, and remember you'll be revisiting this information during each Iteration. However, do recognize the power of having done this work together collaboratively with the client. The more you can make the mini-planning workshops feel like a team effort to build understanding and less like a classic interview, the better.

Gemba

Gaining a shared understanding through whiteboarding is a great start. But hearing about a process is very different from experiencing a process. Let's talk about Gemba.

What is Gemba? Gemba is a Lean term that means, "going to where the work is done and opening our eyes." Sometimes it's translated as "the place where value is created."

It's important because it draws a distinction between learning about an area and physically experiencing it. In organizations which have committed themselves to Lean, managers and executives are encouraged to take routine "Gemba Walks" so they can see for themselves how work actually occurs.

On a Gemba Walk, managers travel to a space to observe work being done and interact with those who are doing it. They don't critique that work or attempt to solve problems. They don't make the walks into presidential visits. They are there to absorb.

In Active Auditing, we strongly recommend at least one, if not more Gemba Walks as part of preparing for any audit. And we recommend it even if the subject area is very familiar to the auditors. In many cases, taking a Gemba Walk with members of the Single Combined Team can be enlightening – you may both see the work in entirely different ways when it is seen together. If at all possible, conduct Gemba Walks in groups.

A series of Gemba Walks lasting a week or more might be necessary to really understand the subject. In one audit of a past organization's water quality laboratory, the subject and issues were so precise and complex, we accepted that doing proper Gemba would take more than a week of immersion.   Far from feeling intrusive, the clients expressed feeling appreciated and were grateful that the auditors bothered to understand them so well.

The nature of a Gemba Walk might seem obvious if we're touring a manufacturing plant. But how does it work if it's accounting or HR, where things happen on computer screens in cubicles?

The purpose is the same, even if there isn't big machinery and inventory to witness. You begin by asking to follow the flow. In Lean, this is usually referred to as the Value Stream. If you are reviewing the recruiting process, for example, have the recruiters walk you through how they experience each step of the process, and don't skip any. Have them show you how the interview process, for example, is done. What is the experience like for the candidate? Where do they wait to be seen? What is their interaction with the front desk? How do they get shuffled around from interview room to interview room?

During your Gemba Walk, phrase most things you utter as questions. Remember, the clients will be studying your reactions intently. Use mindful language and broadcast trust. Don't take notes, except in the most minimal form. This isn't an interview, this is an experience.

Focus on the process and not the people involved. A key Lean principle is "respect for people." Show them deep respect as they show you their work. Remember, they likely spend more time here than they do with their spouses. You may see potential observations during Gemba, but keep them to yourself. You'll need to validate them with facts later anyway, so don't ruin the free flow of information now. Most of what you see in a Gemba Walk will only suggest avenues of inquiry, it won't provide you with proper support for a finding.

Be kind. Smile. Shake hands. Thank everyone you meet for their time and insights.

It doesn't matter whether you do a Gemba Walk before or after a mini-planning workshop.

Don't misuse Gemba. A classic landmine I've seen auditors detonate with Gemba is to use things that are said during a Gemba Walk as audit evidence. This is a sin for two reasons. First, you've given the impression the discussion is casual, and you later pin a finding on casual dialog. That's unacceptably weak audit support. Second, word will get out. Gemba from then on will be a guarded experience, with clients mostly keeping their mouths shut.

During World War II, when the codebreakers of Bletchley Park broke the Enigma code of the Nazis, they realized very early that if they took direct action on any intel that could only have been gotten by breaking the code, the jig would be up. The Nazis would invent a new code and they'd be back to square one. Information from Gemba is like intel from Enigma. If you think you've discovered something important from a Gemba Walk, a wise auditor will seek a secondary way to validate it – and never quote the Gemba Walk as the source.

6. Risk Assessment

Standards 2210.A1 and 2210.A2 of the *International Standards for the Professional Practice of Internal Auditing* state,

2210.A1 – Internal auditors must conduct a preliminary assessment of the risks relevant to the activity under review. Engagement objectives must reflect the results of this assessment.

2210.A2 – Internal auditors must consider the probability of significant errors, fraud, noncompliance, and other exposures when developing the engagement objectives.

However, the method and form of risk assessment aren't defined. There are any number of ways to conduct risk assessments, and it seems I learn a new one at every conference I attend.

The textbook *Internal Auditing: Risk & Advisory Services* offers a reasonably simple brainstorming process for conducting a risk assessment, which many audit teams use. For each process chunk, it involves actively brainstorming the barriers which might prevent that process chunk from achieving its objectives.

Active Auditing deviates from this guidance only slightly. The textbook describes that the process would be "optimized" if individuals involved in the process participate. However, it goes on to say that experienced auditors should be able to conduct the risk assessment process without the assistance of the clients.

On this point, taking onboard lessons from Lean and Agile, we disagree and suggest that the clients *must* be involved in the engagement-level risk assessment process. Eventually the results of the risk assessment will drive and support the contents of the audit program and form the "so what" statements of any future observations. Therefore, involving the Business Owner and key Client Team Members in the risk assessment is critical to Pillar One – Energetic Collaboration.

Of course, when setting Shared Ground Rules for a joint risk assessment exercise, whatever form it takes, make sure you establish that final determination of risk for the audit is a responsibility of the auditors. It falls into the category of a non-negotiable because the auditors, specifically the Audit Owner, represent the "voice of the customer" (e.g., the board).

Iterative Risk Assessment

In an Active Audit, you'll do a risk assessment exercise at the beginning of the engagement and at the end of each Iteration, before starting the next.

At the end of each Iteration, you'll be asking the following:

1. What is the priority of each business process in the next Iteration, based on what I learned from the last? Does anything need to come out or be added?
2. Have I discovered new risks I should cover in the next Iteration?
3. Have I learned information that makes old risks less relevant?
4. Does any audit work from earlier Iterations change the way we should conduct audit work in the next Iteration?

It's certainly possible that your initial risk assessment remains relevant and no adjustment for the next Iteration is necessary. If so, make no changes.

Visual Risk Assessment

We recommend that you take the opportunity of the risk assessment to work both collaboratively and visually.

One way to do so is to start with the whiteboard charts you developed in the mini-planning workshops. In a workshop-like setting, ask the client to rate the most crucial elements, from their point of view, to achievement of their and the organization's business objectives. This can be done a number of ways. One common technique is through an "affinity diagram."

Constructing an affinity diagram is simple.

Continuing with the whiteboard diagrams produced previously, ask each participant in the risk assessment exercise to mark a dot next to the areas they consider most critical to business objective achievement. It's usually best to limit their allotment of dots to some number proportionate to the number of activities on the chart – perhaps no more than 5 dots per client participant. This forces them to choose. They can think of the chunks any way they wish. It wouldn't be surprising to see a client participant draw a circle around a group of business processes and declare them all dotted, with one dot. It's okay. You're capturing their understanding of importance, in their terms.

We've done this exercise with sticky notes, markers, and small adhesive colored dots, and in other ways. It doesn't matter what tool is used.

The auditors involved then do the same thing – placing dots next to the process chunks they view as most important to achievement of organizational objectives. Collating the results, you discuss why certain processes rated highly and others less so. Explore the differences between how the auditors thought of importance compared to the clients. In the end, you've made several steps towards greater mutual purpose and you've accomplished much of your required risk assessment.

7. Draft Control Objectives

Control Objectives (COs) are brief statements of "what good looks like" for each major section of an audit. They finish the sentence, "When things are going just the way we want, it would look like this…" They are written in the positive, meaning they describe the target state – what we want.

In many ways, COs are equivalent to the classic audit criteria. They represent "what should be." The more specific you can get when writing them, the fewer conflicts you'll have later. However, don't shy away from COs that are descriptive and hard to quantify. These are often the most value-added kinds of COs. Just realize early on that non-quantitative COs are harder to defend empirically. If you've done a good job generating mutual purpose, you can still test and write observations based on difficult-to-measure COs.

You construct the COs out of the raw material you collected in the mini-planning workshops, Gemba, and the risk assessment activities. COs can be written at a tactical or strategic level. The more you write them, the better you'll get.

Some possible COs from our example HR audit might include:

- 100% of employee personnel files contain completed Form I-9s with proper supporting documentation (driver's license image, etc.).
- Policies are clear and communicated regarding the use of social media in the candidate evaluation process.
- Pre-employment drug testing is done 100% of the time in accordance with approved policies and applicable law.
- Policies are in place to govern negotiations with potential new hires, and they are applied consistently.
- Interviewing processes are fair, unbiased, and defensible.

Each of these COs, in practice, is likely to have several sub-bullets that further refine "what good looks like."

When you believe you have a reasonably complete set of COs, it's time to do Pillar One and share them for discussion with the clients. Meet with the Governance Layer Owner and Business Owner and confirm that they agree that these are the right COs.

We recommend having them provide affirmative agreement – sign a physical copy, send an email, etc. Don't let the client get away with some version of, "These look mostly correct, but I reserve the right to change my mind later." That's a trap that will spring later when you bring forward an observation and they disavow the validity of the associated CO.

Sometimes they will call out certain COs and declare them to be good ideas, but not standards against which they believe they should be held. Deciding which COs will represent the "measuring stick" in an audit is a balancing act. Auditors have an obligation to point out risks. But taken too far, that can become dictation to management.

While just like in risk assessment, defining COs is ultimately the responsibility of the auditors, as the "voice of the customer" you can damage mutual purpose if you hold too strongly to a CO that doesn't have sturdy support. Put it aside, for now. Come back to it later. As you execute Iterations, you may learn information that changes its criticality (either in your mind or in the client's).

After all, Lean teaches that until a business process has been subjected to continuous improvement attention at least five times, it likely still retains unacceptable levels of waste – or in audit terms, control weakness.

So, even in internal audits, it is sometimes best to take what you can and return to fight another day.

8. Build the Draft Audit Program

Active Auditing uses audit programs just as in traditional auditing – but, of course, we apply the Pillars of Energetic Collaboration, Iterative Execution, and Visual Management. Below, we offer one way to assemble the component parts of an audit program. Every internal audit function I know does this differently, and this approach isn't necessarily unique to Active Auditing. However, it does ensure that we understand why we are doing every fieldwork step before we plan to do it. And it breaks the work into definable parts that we can manage using Lean & Agile techniques.

Feel free to define your audit program however works for you, keeping in mind that it will be useful both for Iterative Execution and Visual Management that you can point to a collection of fieldwork steps and relate them to a larger group.

Control Objectives & Fieldwork Steps

The easiest way to think of Control Objectives and fieldwork steps is to create two columns on a page.

The left column contains the list of Control Objectives. In a medium-sized audit there will likely be 20-30, depending on how detailed you choose to get. The largest audit I've run using Active principles had 75, and they were at a strategic level, with 3-5 sub-objectives providing additional description for each. Others lasted a week and had only 10.

The right column contains the fieldwork activities or tests you imagine can help determine whether each Control Objective is working as expected. Often, there are several fieldwork activities for each Control Objective.

For example, using the Control Objective from our HR example that describes "100% of employee personnel files contain completed Form I-9s," the obvious test would be to pull a sample of new hire personnel files from the last year, and then review the files for proper I-9 documents.

Audit Program Example

Control Objective	Fieldwork Step
3. Talent Acquisition – Recruiting **3.1. Legal Awareness** – All HR staff and 100% of hiring managers are trained in employment law, before being allowed to hire.	**3.1. Legal Awareness** 3.1.1. Review training records to determine how HR ensures all hiring managers and HR recruiting staff are trained. 3.1.2. Select a sample of 10 recruitments in last year and validate via training records, that all participating hiring managers were trained.
3.2. Screen/ Filtering – Processes for filtering candidates are documented, legal, and consistently applied- whether performed by HR or the hiring manager.	**3.2. Screen/Filtering** 3.2.1 Review SOPs and policies related to screening. 3.2.2 Interview lead recruiter and two recruiters separately to understand how SOPs are applied – compare and evaluate.
3.3. Interviewing – Interviewing processes are fair, unbiased, and legally defensible.	**3.3. Interviewing** 3.3.1 Review SOPs and hiring manager training materials for Interviewing. 3.3.2 Interview lead recruiter and two recruiters separately to understand how interview SOPs are applied – be mindful for fairness, bias, and legal issues.
3.4. Social Media – Policies are clear and communicated regarding the use of social media in the candidate evaluation process.	**3.4. Social Media** 3.4.1 Review social media policies and compare to best practice.

On the other hand, verifying that interviewing processes are "fair, unbiased, and defensible" will likely take interviews of the recruiters who guide hiring managers, reviewing personnel policies, and perhaps sitting through training routinely provided to hiring managers regarding their duties. Further, if your risk assessment suggests this subject has significant risks, maybe you've heard that the organization has been sued for this in the past, you might also choose to dig into your organization's legal complaint history to understand weaknesses and gaps.

All these planned fieldwork steps get written in the right column adjacent to their associated Control Objective.

When both columns are filled and there are reasonable fieldwork steps attached to each Control Objective, you've got your first draft audit program. They don't have to be perfect, but they should be as good a plan as you can muster at the beginning. Before each Iteration you are going to reevaluate and revise based on what you've learned.

I find it best to build out an entire draft audit program at the start, recognizing that it will get revised. It's difficult to do reasonable Iteration planning if you don't have at least one version of a complete audit program.

Drafting a full starter audit program can also help ensure compliance with professional standards. Standard 2240.A1 of the *International Standards for the Professional Practice of Internal Auditing* requires that, "The work program must be approved prior to its implementation, and any adjustments approved promptly." While a pure Agile approach to auditing might defer development of a full scope audit program to each Iteration, meeting this standard is easier if you build one for approval at the start. Then, as you revise after each Iteration, get the refinements approved. This seems easier to track.

Lastly, because some audit work requires data with lengthy lead times, having at least one version of the full audit program allows you and the client to anticipate.

Visible Fieldwork Steps

In an Active Audit, fieldwork steps are going to be visible to your clients. You want their help leading you to information, so why be cagey about the step? Let them support you.

We recommend going as far as posting the fieldwork steps on a wall, so you can talk about them together with the clients. On one audit we went as far as printing them on a plotter and hanging the 3'x4' sheet of paper in my office.

Of course, you could just send them a copy via email, which for many auditors would be radical enough. However, Lean teaches us that the moment of shared experience is critical. Being able to talk, in a half-circle, about the upcoming steps is worth 10 emails with the audit program attached.

Until the clients give you some reason not to trust them, the better gamble is to enlist them to help you.

9. Engagement Iteration Planning

Once you have your draft audit program, it's time to lay out a reasonable schedule of Iterations. Again, all of this revisable, but we do our best to develop a rational plan at the outset. In Agile terms, this Engagement Iteration Plan is analogous to a "release schedule," which represents a master schedule assembled from multiple Sprints.

We begin by reviewing the audit program, looking for reasonable groupings that are efficient for both the auditors and the clients. We're looking for reasonable groupings of Control Objectives and their associated fieldwork steps that best:

- Maximize the availability of auditor and client staff
- Make efficient use of client time
- Decrease the number of occasions the auditors have to refresh their understanding of a subject area
- Avoid packing more work into each Iteration than can be done without expediting or rushing
- Anticipate lengthy lead times for data or interview availability
- Deliver completed audit work by the end of each Iteration

Agile purists will argue that we should keep the Iteration cycle the same and vary the work assigned to each Iteration. That might work, but it ignores the highly variable nature of audit work. It also ignores that audit work usually has an ongoing need for significant interaction with and information from the client, which Agile software development typically does not.

For most Agile software projects, client interaction occurs before and after each Sprint. During the Sprint, the clients back off and let the developers build.

Conversely, because audit iterations directly involve the clients, it's better to assign fieldwork steps respecting the client's time and in a fashion that is logical to them. So, if an Iteration needs to be three or four weeks because that best balances the considerations above, we recommend flexing to match, even if the Iterations are of different lengths.

To illustrate using our HR audit, perhaps we have decided that of the 55 Control Objectives being tested, 25 of them involve staff on the recruiting team. We estimate that doing fieldwork steps for all 25 Control Objectives in one Iteration is too much. So, we look for ways to maximize the time efficiency of the recruiting staff. Noticing that 10 Control Objectives primarily involve three specific staff members and the rest involve five others, we lay out our Iteration schedule to take three weeks to cover the 10 Control Objectives and four to cover the remaining 15. That way we contain the time needed with each group and aren't subjecting all eight recruiters to seven weeks of audit attention.

In real life, it's often a bit more complicated due to vacations and other conflicts, but we do our best to create a workable initial Engagement Iteration Plan that covers the entire set of fieldwork steps. We do this knowing that we'll revisit the plan and fieldworks steps at each Iteration – refining them, changing them, or even removing them – based on what we've learned.

Iteration Capacity Planning

Everywhere I go, audit leaders struggle with capacity planning. Some operate elaborate hours and usage calculation tools. Others take their best guess. I seldom encounter audit leaders who report that any of these tools work well for them.

The problem seems to be centered on the inherent variability of audit work. Auditors are generally obligated to follow the information to where it leads, to pull on "strings in the sand" and see where they go. Sometimes that means selecting additional samples, setting up additional interviews, or having reports and data analytics produced that weren't originally anticipated. When an auditor is hot on the trail, it's hard to know when to reel in the work for the sake of the schedule.

We also struggle with client responsiveness, which generates scheduling variability.

The challenge gets somewhat easier with repetitive and limited-complexity audits, but determining how much work a given auditor should be able to knock out in a day or week seems to stump audit leadership the world over.

Agile software development offers several techniques for this, which I've tried with limited result.

One Agile software technique attempts to estimate "Story Points" for a given feature that will be coded and tested during a Sprint. Story Points are an assigned value of time and effort to complete an individual piece of work. They don't have meaning except in context with the Story Points assigned to other features, which are added together to determine the total number of Story Points for that Sprint. That's the demand side of the equation.

On the supply side, the development team assigned to the Sprint calculates the number of Story Points it believes it can complete during the Sprint. This is often called the team's velocity. The totals are compared and adjustments are made to match the work to the team's velocity.

When done well, as each Sprint is completed, the team's actual realized velocity is calculated and, for the next Iteration, adjusted up or down. Perhaps for the last two Sprints the team moved quickly and ran out of features to code and test a day early. This argues for recalculating the team's velocity and setting it higher. As a result, the team would be assigned more Story Points' worth of work in the next Iteration.

Some Agile software teams do a similar exercise and attempt to count person-hours or minutes and add them up to match the available hours in the Iteration.

Other Agile techniques for estimating capacity include the *Team Estimating Game* and *Planning Poker*. We won't go into all the Agile capacity planning techniques in use here. They can be researched easily online. They each can be useful for turning complete guesses into somewhat more informed and well-considered guesses. Their effectiveness in an audit context depends on the degree to which the audit team can predict the amount of time each fieldwork step will take – allowing for variability.

During most of my career, that predictability has been elusive because the issues at hand weren't highly repetitive and so the fieldwork steps to evaluate them were highly customized. Moreover, it is impossible to predict the nature or number of observations that will result from the work, and experienced auditors know that issues that lead to observations unpredictably eat up time.

To deal with these challenges, Active Auditing steps back, doesn't try to get too technical, and takes a broad view of capacity planning.

Recognizing that the Active Auditing approach is intended to be flexible, we make our best estimate of what we can get done within the confines of an Iteration and then rely on Energetic Collaboration to shrink the client-side variables and Visual Management (discussed in Pillar Three) to make actual progress visible in real time. Then at each Iteration we check ourselves and ask how good our initial estimates were.

True Lean masters will likely find this approach unfulfilling. However, I've yet not found a way to make the inherently exploratory nature of (most of my) audit work act like a properly smoothed process flow. For audit work that is highly repeatable, eliminating Mura (unevenness in operation) becomes more possible.

This flexible capacity planning is done by the Audit Owner first setting a "strawman" Engagement Iteration Schedule for the entire audit program, based on their best estimate of capacity. This is followed by an Iteration Planning Session. An Iteration Planning Session typically includes the Audit Owner, Audit Team Members, and Audit Oversight, who scour the strawman schedule looking for things that could throw it off track.

Iteration Planning Sessions are best done by a group, perhaps with the audit program on a projector screen or monitor. In the session, the team asks the following questions for each fieldwork step:

1. Is there anything about this step that we imagine will take more time than might have been originally expected?
2. Is there any way to accelerate this step and still have it be useful?
3. Is there anything we can do for this step to ensure it takes as much time as we expect (e.g., advance document requests, additional explanation to the client, more research)?
4. Is this step truly necessary to determine whether the Control Objective is being achieved?

With this exercise, we're trying to surface new information that wasn't in mind when the strawman Engagement Iteration Plan was originally created. And we're doing so with the combined thinking of the team, not just the Audit Owner or Audit Oversight. Through this process, we often find that members of the team have very different understandings of the fieldwork steps. Some think a step will be quick, while others envisioned it being deep and extensive. We're also trying to surface risks that might impact completion of the step which weren't considered when the Engagement

Iteration Plan was built. This helps hone the estimate.

It can be easy to spend too much time in an Iteration Planning Session. The team will revisit it again after each Iteration, so it's wisest to make the best determination you can in a short time and move on.

Before each Iteration, the team should ask "How good was the last estimate?" and "Is there any way to get better?"

What does an Engagement Iteration Plan look like?

We'll discuss how to present and manage the Engagement Iteration Plan in the next section on Visual Management.

For now, the Engagement Iteration Plan itself is nothing more than time-boxed dates assigned to each section of the audit program. Each Control Objective, along with its associated fieldwork steps, is assigned to an Iteration.

We don't recommend creating a separate document for the Plan. Adding a column or notation to the audit program is sufficient. However, it is wise to keep an updated copy of the Engagement Iteration Plan each time it is revised. This makes it possible to evaluate how the Plan has changed over time and to learn from it.

PHASE - Fieldwork

Based on your Engagement Iteration Plan, it's time to begin interviewing, mapping, testing, and documenting the audit work in workpapers. This is the good stuff — the "meat" of the audit.

Every audit team does the mechanics of fieldwork differently, and like planning, teams can continue to use the method that has been comfortable in the past. Fieldwork and testing are done in an Active Audit essentially the same as in traditional audits. The biggest difference is the iterative approach.

10. Iterations (A through ?)

Start with Iteration A and continue, treating each Iteration as a mini-audit, performing the following steps:

a)   Interviews & Testing
b)   Frequent Client Validation
c)   Workpaper Review
d)   Workpaper Approval
e)   Observations
f)   Reevaluation
g)   Plan for Next Iteration

Interviews & Testing

Perform fieldwork as you would do any other audit. Execute the fieldwork steps. Pull samples, conduct interviews, analyze data, and substantively test. Document the work as normal, using whatever workpaper process makes sense. Keep in mind the 7 Collaborative Essentials from Pillar One.

Frequent Client Validation

Energetic Collaboration in this context means bringing potential issues to the clients as early as possible, often even before you're certain of the facts. This carries some risk of "crying wolf" too early, but remember we are hoping to be well led by our clients. And we will have explained to the clients during Shared Ground Rules setting that we will err on the side of communicating, even if it sometimes results in false positives.

We are attempting to avoid wasted time for everyone on the Single Combined Team.

Many auditors will spend significant time in a spiral of self-checking before engaging the client for more information. Often they find it easier to query more data than to get up and go talk to a member of the client team. Resist that urge. Reach out earlier than may be typical.

Auditors also have a tendency to want to build an airtight case because the risk of being wrong is intolerable. Go ahead – implement Essential #5 (Vulnerable Auditors) and communicate it with appropriate context before building an indisputable case.

A valuable technique is to telegraph potential observations at Standups. This is a wise idea because it tends to summon additional information that can break the spiral. Use Mindful Language and Broadcast Trust when you do so.

Workpaper Review

Lean teaches that "batching" is never as efficient as continuous flow. The classic demonstration of this principle involves assembling ten people, five to a side, at a conference table for a race. Each side is handed a stack of sticky notes and told they will be signing their first name on each. They will then pass the note down the line. The task for each sticky note is complete when it shows five signatures done in sequence.

The task is the same for both sides; however, the first person on one side is told to batch their work. In other words, they must sign 8 sticky notes before handing those notes to the next person. The other side is instructed to sign one note and pass it on, then sign another… and so on.

A stop watch starts and for 60 seconds both sides of the table attempt to process as many sticky notes as they can. The side with the greatest number of stickies with five sequential signatures at the end of 60 seconds wins a prize.

The continuous flow side always wins.

This lesson can be applied to workpaper review and approval. To the greatest extent possible, in Active Auditing we attempt to complete workpaper review in real time and not allow workpapers to languish. Ideally, by the end of each Iteration, the workpapers will have been reviewed by the Audit Oversight role, comments returned, and refinements made.

In traditional auditing, many auditors struggle to have workpapers completely done and approved before observations are issued. Though arguably no observation should ever be provided to the client unless it is fully supported by audit evidence, it's easy to get "upside down." Since workpapers aren't client-facing, they are often seen as backroom administrative work – work that should be done on our own time and not during the part of the audit that involves the client.

Moreover, audit managers often struggle to be attentive to workpaper review. This leads to stagnant inventories of unreviewed workpapers. Even if every issued observation is checked and supported, these inventories still mean the knowledge embedded in them is growing stale. A workpaper comment provided in real-time can be addressed by an auditor whose understanding of the subject is still fresh. A comment from a hoard of unreviewed workpapers is a version of the Lean Waste "extra processing" and represents rework as the auditor reacquaints themselves with the subject.

Active Auditing intends to produce workpapers in a continuous flow, so they can be reviewed and approved using an unbatched approach. This probably requires structuring the audit differently. We recommend making the Control Objective the unit of flow. So when all the fieldwork steps associated with that Control Objective are complete, the Control Objective can be marked ready for workpaper review. This progress is tracked on the Visual Control Board, which is discussed in Pillar Three.

Of course, it's not always possible to achieve real-time review of workpapers. Sometimes the topics are complex and questions can't be answered rapidly. Nevertheless, this is what Lean calls the target state. By seeking to complete workpaper reviews within each Iteration, we have a greater chance of arriving at the end of the audit without a lengthy stockpile.

Workpaper Approval

The second core value of the Agile Manifesto written by the seventeen founding members of the Agile Alliance is "Working software over comprehensive documentation." This core value was written to combat what was seen as a lengthy and expensive devotion to documenting software prior to delivery. Comprehensive documentation of specifications, requirements, test plans, and approvals had grown to be the norm and was seen to be causing lengthy delays. Also, it wasn't seen as directly linkable to customer value.

Further, a tenet of Lean is to drive as much non-value-added (NVA) work from every business process as possible. According to Lean, value-added (VA) work must meet all three of the following criteria:

- The work transforms something toward completion
- The work is done right the first time (e.g., not a rework step)
- The customer cares that the work is done (and/or would pay for it to be done)

Some NVA work is necessary for legal or regulatory reasons, but it still is understood to not be adding value… from the customer's point of view.

Active Auditing recommends keeping both the Agile core value and the concept of NVA in mind when balancing the risk of challenge to the audit work with the cost of documentation (both in terms of resources and time). It's a balance every audit team has to find for itself.

Clearly, workpapers (calculations, analysis, etc.) that transform facts from being merely data into insights and observations are adding value. Likewise, workpapers that the clients would find useful in their operations (process maps, dashboard data, etc.) could be considered VA. Completed and approvable workpapers in an Active Audit should be as VA as possible.

In some environments, risk of challenge is high and can extend into legal or regulatory exposures. Compliance and Sarbanes-Oxley work is often typified by higher risk. However, for many of us, once reviewed and approved, workpapers are generally never read again.

Observations

Observations are not "findings" in Active Auditing. Observations are discussion items. They're noted gaps between what was expected and what was. In Lean A3 terms, they are the space between the current state and the target state. There is enough there that it is valuable to write it down, but writing it down doesn't make it true.

The father of baseball umpires, Bill Klem, once said, "It ain't nothing till I call it."

So too an observation "ain't nothing until it is discussed with the client." It's not a fact, an issue, a problem, or a control failure until the facts are communicated and an opportunity to receive additional information and context occurs. Only then can it be regarded as an issue or finding.

While there are many ways to deliver the results of an audit, Pillar One requires that the clients have their say before the ink is allowed to dry into a finding.

Observations must have workpaper support, but in Active Auditing we encourage sharing the potential observation with the client as soon it can hold together under scrutiny.

According to the Agile Alliance, the first of 12 Agile Principles is, "Our highest priority is to satisfy the customer through early and continuous delivery of valuable software." Active Auditing modifies this principle to make early and continuous delivery of insights and information to the clients a top priority. "Speed-to-market" for software. "Speed-to-improvement" for audit work. If it's worth mentioning as a potential finding, it's worth mentioning quickly, so the gap can be closed and the risk mitigated.

Every audit team will need to strike the right balance between delivering an unsupported observation too early and waiting too long. When given a choice, Active Auditing recommends erring on the side of early.

Reevaluation

The final principle of the Agile Alliance's 12 Agile Principles is, "At regular intervals, the team reflects on how to become more effective, then tunes and adjusts its behavior accordingly." Likewise, all models of Lean teach reflection and reassessment to get better constantly.

In an Active Audit, before we begin the next Iteration, we stop and reevaluate. In Agile Scrum, this is usually called a Retrospective. It can be done with the clients or not, depending on how effectively the team seems to be working together.

Many Agile Scrum crusaders will likely argue that the entire Single Combined Team must be involved in the reevaluation session after each Iteration. We don't find that necessary. Unlike in software development, the clients have been closely involved throughout the Iteration as part of Standups and other interactions. It's often too much to ask to require participation after each Iteration. After all, we'll conduct a Retrospective session at the end of the audit and include everyone then.

Nevertheless, we recommend including the Business Owner, if possible, in a scheduled reevaluation session to discuss the following:

1. What challenges were encountered in the last Iteration and what Countermeasures can we install to help with those challenges?
2. What were the bottlenecks in the last Iteration?
3. How accurate was our capacity estimate, and what adjustments need to be made?
4. Did we get appropriate and effective involvement from all members of the Single Combined Team? Particularly, did we get enough attention from the Governance Layer Owner, Chief Audit Executive, and Audit Oversight roles?

Plan for Next Iteration

Armed with insights from the reevaluation session, the auditor team holds an Iteration Planning Session. In this session, the auditors discuss the following:

- Have we learned anything that causes our original risk assessment to change?
- Does a change in our risk assessment mean we need to reexamine

the Engagement Iteration Plan?
- Do we need to change, reorder, or cancel any fieldwork intended in the next Iteration?
- Does something need to move to a different Iteration?
- Is the timing of the next Iteration reasonable?

The result of this session is a revised plan for the next Iteration and it's possible the Engagement Iteration Plan will also need to be modified. Be sure to record these changes for later reference, not losing the previous Plans. Also, be sure to inform the clients of any changes. Depending on magnitude, this could occur at the next Standup. However, if the changes are sizeable, perhaps adjusting the expected completion date by weeks or months, it's probably wise for the Chief Audit Executive to inform the Governance Layer Owner directly first.

Rinse and Repeat

You'll repeat the above steps for each Iteration, adjusting and installing Countermeasures appropriate to the moment, getting better with each round.

A word of caution, however. While you can get better with each Iteration, that improvement is heavily dependent on the involved members of the team remaining the same. If Iteration A involves five client members, but Iteration B only carries forward one client member from Iteration A, the team will start back at the beginning. Even if your audit team remains essentially the same, the next Iteration will only get partial benefit from the experience of the previous one.

To combat this effect, we recommend increasing the involvement of the members of Iteration B before the end of Iteration A. Have them attend Standups more frequently. Monitor their attendance. If necessary, take some time after a Standup to get them up to speed.

Psychologist Bruce Tuckman first came up with the memorable phrase "forming, storming, norming, and performing" in his 1965 article, "Developmental Sequence in Small Groups." It represents the path that most teams follow on their way to high performance. Unfortunately, when significant pieces of a team change, the team bounces back to the beginning.

This is true of the progression of the Single Combined Team during an audit, and also your progression as an audit function introducing Active

Auditing to your organization. Following your first Active Audit, those who participated will be veterans of the approach. However, your next audit clients are newborns to it. Respect their need to progress through the stages.

Avoid too many occasions where you reference your last Single Combined Team's progress and success. Knowing that last year's high school football team won the championship doesn't really help this year's players if most of the starters on that team graduated, and hearing the tales gets old.

PHASE - Reporting

Standard 2440 of the *International Standards for the Professional Practice of Internal Auditing* states, "The chief audit executive must communicate results to the appropriate parties." The associated interpretation states, "The chief audit executive is responsible for reviewing and approving the final engagement communication before issuance and for deciding to whom and how it will be disseminated. When the chief audit executive delegates these duties, he or she retains overall responsibility."

How each audit team fulfills this duty varies wildly. Some write extensive and detailed reports that contain every last detail. Others contain their reports to just the fundamental or major findings. Indeed, many audit teams grade their audits and many more do not. In one global audit team of which I was a part, the rule was no more than 10 pages, regardless of the issues found. Their customers, the regional and global audit committees, wouldn't read any more than that. I have several colleagues who deliver their reports exclusively in PowerPoint form, because their audit committee won't read even 10 pages of prose.

When you are immersed in the religions of Lean and Agile, the reporting phase presents some fascinating choices. How you make them depends on your environment and, more than anything, what your customers want. And, who's the customer? That's right, the board.

Report Choices

In an Active Audit, how you structure your reporting phase depends on how you make the following choices.

"Issue & Respond" vs. "Management Agreed"

In my career, I've almost exclusively operated a reporting process referred to as the "management agreed" approach. This means the auditors negotiate the facts, risks, and mitigating actions with the clients before publishing them as findings in a written report.

A finding begins as a noted gap (perhaps interview results or a tick mark appearing in a workpaper test matrix) between what we expected to find and what we found. After additional validation, it progresses to being a written observation. As described above, when an observation's facts and context are confirmed, it becomes a finding and the client assumes an obligation to do one of two things –

A.   Formulate a mitigating action plan to fix it with an owner and target completion date, or

B.   Accept the risk.

Only a Governance Layer Owner may accept risks. And in some organizations, the CEO retains that authority to themselves alone.

The auditors may offer a recommended action plan to the client, but the client is under no obligation to accept that plan.

If the auditors and client reach an impasse and can't agree on the facts, risks, or mitigating action plans, the auditors will report that impasse in their report, but every effort will have been made beforehand to avoid a deadlock.

In only one assurance engagement of my career did I ever reach a full-on impasse with a client. I've come close many times, but in this case, the stakes were high and the Governance Layer Owner didn't see the situation our way. She fought the findings and the board got involved. As unfortunate as that was, it is how the system is supposed to work.

All in all, for most of my career the customer has preferred that their auditors and the clients do the hard work of negotiating before results were presented. When the process works, reports represent a closed loop.

Issue found - options identified - plan implemented - risk mitigated.

Only if that loop is interrupted, if it fails to close, does the board need to get involved.

This isn't how all audit shops function, however. Many publish their findings and then expect a published written response from management. Often responses come in the form of rebuttals, but even when they are issue-

and solution-focused, the customer is left with two stories to read, two versions of the truth. One written by the auditors and one by the clients.

There are benefits to this approach. The auditors don't need to negotiate, they just lay the facts, as they understand them, on the table. And the auditors aren't required to judge the quality of response. That role is left to the board.

Nevertheless, there are significant risks to an "issue & respond" process. Every time the auditors are proven incorrect in public, and it will happen, their credibility goes down. Worse, the board is arguably in the least capable position to understand who has the facts most correct. Boards are seldom close enough to judge.

Not all chief audit executives have a choice of which process they use. Some are organizationally structured such that issue & respond is the only way they can provide their results. Government auditors are often forced to use this approach.

Issue & respond can seriously damage the sense of mutual purpose that is necessary to effectively employ Active Auditing. The damage is almost irreparable if the written findings pass back and forth in a public setting. If the back and forth can be kept within the Single Combined Team, it is possible to maintain mutual purpose, but it's difficult. Doing so requires a huge amount of emphasis on validating facts and risks within the Iteration and telegraphing what will appear in the issued report before it appears. To retain mutual purpose, this work must be done early.

For this reason, we recommend Active Audits use a form of management agreed approach whenever possible.

Speed & Depth of Response

In an Active Audit, by the end of each Iteration, ideally workpapers will have been reviewed and approved, observations will have been issued, and agreed management actions received. This is the closest an audit can come to sellable software at the end of each Sprint.

Whether this is reasonable to expect depends on two things: 1) complexity of the finding, and 2) the decision making maturity of the client team.

However, we can't subscribe to Lean teachings and simultaneously expect clients to provide knee-jerk and unconsidered action plans to complex findings. Lean teaches us three crucial things that are applicable to mitigating action plans.

1. **Respect for People** – The people doing the work must solve the problems for themselves.

2. **Experimentation** – The potential solutions need to be tried in-process before we know if they are better than what came before.

3. **Cause Statements Are Dangerous** – Root cause analysis is a lengthy process that requires, at minimum, that "why" be asked five times. Auditors can help by providing information on how a failure occurred, but we muddy the waters when we guess at cause.

These lessons combine to make detailed agreed actions for even marginally complex findings almost impossible to collect from clients quickly. And that truth collides with our desire to execute the audit iteratively.

Again, the required depth of response is not always in the control of the chief audit executive. Many audit committees demand fairly detailed commitments quickly. For very high-risk issues that's probably warranted. However, it carries a counter-risk of slapping bandages on problems. "Field tourniquets" are inherently anti-Lean. Taiichi Ohno would roll over in his grave to hear of it.

If it doesn't seem reasonable to obtain well-considered mitigating action plans within a single Iteration, a compromise is to require them to be received by the end of the next. This allows time for the clients to discuss potential solution approaches, while not extending the wait time unreasonably.

We recommend discussing the subject of agreed actions with your audit committee and/or board as you transition to Active Auditing and again at least annually, likely during the annual audit planning process. Remind them that a well-crafted mitigating action need not require a detailed response. Instead it should possess the following:

1. Owner
2. Commitment to develop a solution
3. Methodology for developing the solution

4.   Expected artifact of an effective solution – what will tell us that the issue is solved?

5.   Target completion date

The specific solution approach isn't as important as the commitment to creating one and the thought process for how it will be developed. Skeptics will accuse me of recommending "a plan to make a plan," and there is some risk of that. Indeed, as a young auditor and consultant it was driven into me that "plans to plan" were copouts. We're letting the clients off the hook. Some clients will view it that way. But that behavior thrives best in traditional auditing, where there isn't mutual purpose.

To Grade or Not to Grade?

I have issued plenty of graded audit reports in my time, with descriptors such as unacceptable or less than adequate. I've graded issues, declaring them fundamental, major, or minor.

By now I hope you'll be quick to point out that grading is another obvious swipe at mutual purpose. It's not focused on continuous improvement – it's intrinsically judging – and it will make it difficult for everyone to see themselves as part of the Single Combined Team. It's hard to visualize a Single Combine Team working together, when one of the parties carries a gavel, dresses in dark robes, and wears a long wig. If you can avoid it, don't grade.

If you can't avoid it, because your customer (the board) has requested this service from their combined team, do it together. You can do it by discussion or you can do it using facilitation techniques like affinity charts or polling. Ideally, you come to consensus. If you can't, it's a reasonable approach to list two grades – the auditor view and the client view. Better a minor difference of reporting than coming to blows over whether an issue is fundamental or major.

Reporting Format

Active Auditing doesn't attempt to dictate any particular reporting approach. As mentioned above, the form of report is often dictated by the audit committee, and a chief audit executive's ability to modify it may be limited. However, both Lean and Agile offer some concepts for consideration when defining a reporting format.

Lean – Customer Defines Value – This principle of Lean reminds us that it should ultimately be the board who decides whether the reporting format is useful to them. Many of us write reports the way we like them and, in passing, ask our boards whether they find them useful. Usually they say yes. But often that's because they don't have any basis for comparison or they're not prepared for the question.

The situation is not entirely unlike customers in a grocery checkout line who get asked, "Did you find everything OK?" Most of us, when asked such a question, just say yes. We figure they don't really want to know and couldn't do anything about it if we gave them an honest answer. So, we smile and say something inoffensive.

A better technique, common to Lean, is to include actual customers on project teams and improvement events, so they can represent the voice of the customer. They become part of the team working on continuously improving. If you have the opportunity, we recommend doing more than just asking casually. Invite members of the audit committee to have a structured discussion about audit reporting and explore the subject.

Agile – Working Software over Comprehensive Documentation – This principle from Agile reminds us to trim down the report and to be on the lookout for overly comprehensive content. Most audit committee members have limited time – they need the salient information quickly.

Lean – A3 Thinking – What's fascinating about an A3 is how parallel it is to the classic five-part audit finding most of us were taught as young auditors. The classic model for writing a finding usually includes condition, criteria, cause, risk/effect, and recommendation/action. The parallels are so close that at one point we considered issuing our observations in A3 format. However, most of our clients hadn't progressed sufficiently on their Lean journey to have found the change useful. Perhaps one day they would. Nevertheless, if you lay an A3 side by side with an IA finding, you get the following translation.

A3 to Internal Audit Translation

LEAN A3 Term	IA Term
Planning — 1. Reason for Action ⟶	Risk
2. Current State ⟶	Condition
3. Target State ⟶	Criteria
4. Gap Analysis ⟶	Observation
5. Solutions Approach ⟶	Recommendation
Doing — 6. Rapid Experiments ⟶	NWIOL
7. Completion Plans ⟶	Management Actions
8. Confirmed State ⟶	Completed Actions
9. Insights ⟶	NWIOL

Interestingly, there are several important components of an A3 which have no parallel in the classic five-part audit finding model. We note them above with the acronym NWIOL, which means No Word in Our Language.

The two untranslatable words are instructive.

The first is Rapid Experiments. Because an A3 is designed not just to report problems, but to manage their resolution, it contains a space for defining what actions we might take, what we expect to see as a result, and then a comparison with the result we actually achieved.

This part of A3 Thinking reminds us that no new action is deemed better than what came before until it's tried and measured. This is a very different mindset from the linear approach of classic auditing where a finding is reported, a plan implemented to fix, and, when the defined action is done, the finding is closed. Properly implemented Lean-based reporting wouldn't close the finding until the outcome is measured and determined to be better than the former current state. Moreover, in a pure Lean environment it wouldn't be closed until the process was producing results within defined tolerances – even if that meant trying something else.

The second untranslatable term is insights. In this box, the human reaction to the work is captured. Simply by caring about it, an A3 goes much further than traditional internal auditing. But more than that, understanding how the action or change is impacting the people is critically important to sustaining continuous improvement. What did they learn from the work? How did it make them feel? What will they be taking with them for their own development or the development of others?

The insights box reminds us that the human aspects of audit work and our relationships with our clients are critical.

To the old-school auditors who find Active Auditing's constant discussion of the human side of the work somewhat difficult to swallow, I offer that it seems to matter to top executives of Toyota, the fifth richest company in the world based on 2017 revenue, at roughly $255 billion.

Lean – Visual Reporting – We'll discuss Visual Management more in Pillar Three. However, in terms of reporting, the principle reminds us that our reports should tell their customers instantly whether the subject area is on track or off. Infographics, red/amber/green matrices, and Harvey Bubble Tables are all useful methods of making the situation clear.

A Harvey Bubble Table shows each Control Objective for the audit and includes with it a Harvey Bubble progress indicator. Harvey Bubbles are similar to Andons, but the meanings of the quadrants are somewhat different.

Harvey Bubble Key

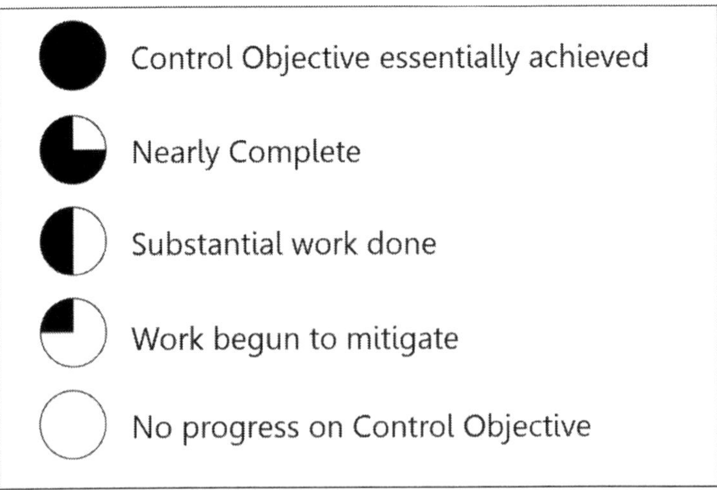

Also, a full Harvey Bubble Table comes in two parts. The first part is likely to appear in the executive summary of the report and the second is probably more appropriate as an appendix. An executive summary Harvey Bubble Table might look like the example:

Example: Harvey Bubble Table

	3.1. Legal Awareness – All HR staff and 100% of hiring managers are trained in employment law, before being allowed to hire.	3.2. Screen/ Filtering – Processes for filtering candidates are documented, legal, and consistently applied- whether performed by HR or the hiring manager.	3.3. Interviewing – Interviewing processes are fair, unbiased, and legally defensible.	3.4. Social Media – Policies are clear and communicated regarding the use of social media in the candidate evaluation process.	3.5. Reference Checks – Policies are clear and communicated regarding reference checking and how it is to be documented	3.6. Scoring – Standardized scoring processes are in place to increase defensibility and avoid legal issues.
3. TALENT - Recruiting						

	4.1. Background Checks – 100% of hired applicants receive a background check appropriate to their position.	4.2. Negotiatns – Policies are in place and followed that govern negotiations with potential new hires, and they are applied consistently.	4.3. Drug Testing – Pre-employment drug-testing is done 100% of the time in accordance with approved policies and applicable law.	4.4. I-9 Forms – 100% of employee personnel files contain completed I-9 forms with the supporting documentation (driver's license image, etc.)	
4. TALENT - Hiring					

	5.1. Total Rewards Philosophy – Compensation philosophy is communicated and comp policies and practices are in-line with the philosophy.	5.2. Comp. Structure – Hierarchy of jobs (grade and placement) is in place and regularly reviewed (at least every 2 years)	5.3. Position Maintenance – Processes are in place and operating on a regular cycle to review each job for appropriate placement in grade and range.	5.4. Other Comp – Policies for changing employ. pay other than by annual merit are in place & followed consistently. HR has effective oversight.	5.5 Equal Pay QC - Regular review and oversight processes are in place to detect disparate treatment in pay.
5. COMPENSATION					

The second portion, which is probably best as an appendix, is a listing of each Control Objective and a few lines describing why it received the Harvey

Bubble it did. It can be done as a table or just a list. It's reference material for the reader who wants to know why, for example, **4.3. Drug Testing** is only half-filled. It should reference the finding that appears elsewhere in the report and offer a one- or two-line summary of the issue.

Though I've never had the need to do this, you could even use color to denote those Control Objectives that are considered higher risk than others. It would be entirely in keeping with Visual Management principles. Problems in **4.3 Drug Testing** could be pretty serious. In the U.S., there are constitutional issues of right to privacy and illegal search and seizure in effect when it comes to pre-employment drug testing. Perhaps the color of the half-filled Harvey Bubble changes to red for those with particularly high remaining risk pending completion of the client's mitigating action plan.

We would argue that Harvey Bubbles are more useful than grades because grades are intrinsically about FYI, rather than FYA (for your information vs. for your action – see next section). We'd also argue that using a technique like Harvey Bubbles in your report acknowledges the five product types discussed in Section One.

To illustrate, you may still offer observations and findings related to a Type Five product (e.g. suggestions), but it wouldn't likely affect the "filled-in-ness" of the Harvey Bubble for that Control Objective. And a Type Two product (e.g. fix is in the works) might be appropriately shown as a ¾ Harvey Bubble, to indicate that there is remaining risk, but it's close to being resolved.

11. Final Agreed Actions

A great deal of what occurs in Steps 11, 12, and 13 depends on how you and your customer made the report choices above. If you are successful obtaining agreed actions within the confines of each Iteration, this step actually belongs in the fieldwork phase.

If you operate an issue & respond process, this step will likely occur after Step 13 – Final Report.

And if you are required to grade issues, you'll want to do so in context with the client and their intended mitigating action plan. After all, if you label an issue as minor, but the client plans on spending significant effort to fix it, you may wish to jointly rethink that grade.

12. Draft Report

I suspect most internal audit shops are in the habit of providing their clients an opportunity to see audit reports prior to final publishing. There is usually no harm in it, and Pillar One essentially requires this step in an Active Audit context.

The biggest question at this stage is usually how much license the clients have to suggest changes. Defining this is good material for the Shared Ground Rules, either at the beginning of the audit or at some point during the first Iteration. We recommend establishing the following:

- Final determination of what appears in the report belongs to the auditors.
- All feedback from the clients that makes the facts more accurate is welcome.
- Style or preference changes aren't welcome, unless they meaningfully change the report's accuracy.
- Whenever possible, the report will give credit for progress and positive examples of good control.

13. Final Report

Only when the final report is published can we consider the audit project complete. It's analogous to move-in day in following a construction project or deployment of new software.

We recommend continuing to Energetically Collaborate all the way to this momentous day and, frankly, beyond until the mitigating action plans are closed. Even if you cut back Standups to once or twice a week after all the Iterations are done and the report is being written, don't abandon them until the final report is issued.

PHASE - Follow-up

Standard 2500.A1 of the *International Standards for the Professional Practice of Internal Auditing* requires that the chief audit executive establish "a follow-up process to monitor and ensure that management actions have been effectively implemented or that senior management has accepted the risk of not taking action." The implementation guidance from the IIA is fairly limited regarding what constitutes an effective monitoring process. It discusses that it "could be a spreadsheet, database, or other tool that contains the prior audit observations, associated corrective action plan, status, and internal audit's confirmation." It also points out that there are typically corrective action plan status reports prepared for senior management and the board.

This leaves us pretty wide latitude for tracking mitigating action plans resulting from an Active Audit. There are lessons from Lean that can help guide a more effective follow-up process.

14. Tracking Action Plans

For the most part, in my career I've used simple spreadsheet solutions for tracking mitigating action plans. When an audit report is published, each of the agreed actions gets copied into an enhanced spreadsheet, which calculates days-till-due and provides a ready spot to add diary notes based on updates from the clients. Usually monthly, a copy of the relevant portions of the database, along with some descriptive metrics (e.g., # of overdue actions) is emailed out to the clients and executive management. It's primarily the client's responsibility to provide updates. IA staff will keep an eye on mitigating action plans that represent particularly high risk, and if they aren't getting completed on time, they'll prompt executive management.

This a largely administrative activity, which barely warrants any attention in internal auditing textbooks and practice guides. However, there is an important Lean lesson that auditors should consider. Not surprisingly, the lesson employs Pillars One and Three.

When an organization on a Lean journey decides to improve a set of business processes, it usually sets up a core team, with an executive sponsor, to guide the effort. The core team will Energetically Collaborate through the effort, defining and directing different kinds of projects to improve the set of business processes. They'll typically hold routine Standups around Visual Control Boards structured for the purpose. Not surprisingly, all of this is strongly similar to the behavior of the Single Combined Team in an Active Audit.

Lean teams seeking to improve business processes will often establish an Obeya. In Japanese the term means "big room," but analogies are often drawn to the bridge of a ship, a war room, or a command center. We'll discuss Obeyas more in Pillar Three, but for now it's most useful to think of them as a commandeered conference room with lots of wall space or a section of hallway. The Obeya will have a Visual Control Board consisting of dashboards, progress charts, and usually a collection of A3s.

You may recall from our Requisite Lean discussion, an A3 is comprised of nine boxes:

Box 1) Reason for Action
Box 2) Current State
Box 3) Target State
Box 4) Gap Analysis
Box 5) Solutions Approach
Box 6) Rapid Experiments
Box 7) Completion Plans
Box 8) Confirmed State
Box 9) Insights

The chief lesson from Lean in this regard is that the core team doesn't disband until Box 8 of their guiding A3 (confirmed state) <u>equals</u> Box 3 (target state). Until they can empirically prove they've not only accomplished the task, but actually changed the current state, they keep working at it. They continue to hold Standups at their Obeya, reviewing their Visual Control Board, and monitoring improvement. Core teams have a number of tools available to create improvement. These include Quick Win (or Just-Do-It) projects, as well as Rapid Improvement Events, 5S Events, Value Stream Mappings (also called Kaizen Events), etc. The core team and executive sponsors define and employ these tools to drive their current state to become their target state (Box 3 = Box 8).

If they've completed all their rapid experiments and all their completion plans have met their due dates, but the confirmed state is not matching the target state, they start again, trying something new. This continues until they match.

This approach is somewhat different from the traditional audit's linear approach to tracking action plans.

It reminds us that whatever action plan tracking approach we employ, it should assume the following:

1. The Single Combined Team (at least its leaders – Governance Layer Owner, Business Owner, Chief Audit Executive, and Audit Owner) doesn't fully disband until all the mitigating action plans for that audit are complete and, more importantly, the confirmed state equals the target state. Some form of routine Standup should continue, though frequency may become bi-weekly or monthly, depending on the action plans.

2. Mitigating action plans may not be successful initially and may need to be changed, retried, and reassessed – i.e., experimentation is encouraged.

15. Celebration & Retrospective

In an Active Audit, in addition to the reevaluation sessions that occur after each Iteration, we recommend holding two post-engagement activities.

The first is a simple celebration. The Single Combined Team just worked hard together to produce an important deliverable for their customer. It's worthy of celebration.

Have a party at your Obeya. Have fake champagne and encourage toasts. Dispense awards – Fastest Data Request, Best Attendance at Standups, Most Helpful Administrative Assistant. Make a big deal out of it.

Our ace-in-the-hole, which you are free to adopt, is that we would purchase a round cake with white icing and ensure that it sat on a black base.

Carrot cakes work well for this. The point is that as you serve slices of cake, you reveal more of the black base, which is evocative of the Andons the group has been working with during the entire audit. It's a good way to laugh at yourself and enjoy a bit of kinship together.

Hold your party whenever you consider yourself done with all the Iterations.

The second post-engagement activity is the Retrospective. This tool is borrowed directly from Agile. Time the Retrospective for shortly after the report is published. The team needs to have experienced the entire cycle up through reporting. This is not an interview, this is a shared team moment of reflection.

There are many suggested formats for Agile Scrum Retrospectives and you are encouraged to try them. Nevertheless, we offer the following guidance:

1. Schedule for 1.5 to 2 hours, and do so shortly after the work is done while everyone's recollections are fresh.
2. Either the Audit Owner or Chief Audit Executive facilitates.
3. Invite as many of the Single Combined Team for all Iterations as possible.
4. Write on a white board the following categories with room to write underneath each:
   a. What should we keep?
   b. What should we get rid of?
   c. What do we want more of?
   d. What do we want less of?
   e. How did we do on our Hearts & Minds Panel?
5. Facilitator works the group, getting them to offer comments for each category and making notes on the whiteboard with markers.
6. At the end of the Retrospective, take a picture of the whiteboard and send out to everyone. Store the picture in IA's workpapers.
7. Auditors meet later to identify one or two suggestions that they commit to implementing in the next audit.
8. Write the commitments on stickies and place on the Visual Control Board for the next audit engagement. Make change.

16. Closing Mitigating Action Plans

Continuing the point described in **14. Tracking Action Plans**, we recommend in an Active Audit that mitigating action plans be closed when the original risk is demonstrably mitigated, not when the task is complete. Close when Box 8 equals Box 3.

It's a bit like when your parent would say, "I didn't tell you to wash your hands, I told you to get your hands clean."

We recommend the auditors gather artifacts which both demonstrate that they washed <u>and</u> that they got their hands clean. While IIA standards indicate that follow-up audit work is often a necessary part of post-engagement monitoring, a better approach is to place that duty on the clients. If you require that data demonstrate mitigating action plans were not only completed, but that they worked, you'll provide much more valuable assurance to your customer.

FOUR

"The most dangerous kind of waste is the
waste we do not recognize."
– Shigeo Shingo

PILLAR THREE: **VISUAL MANAGEMENT**

It's 9:30 a.m. on a Tuesday in the middle of Iteration B of the human resources audit. The auditors are gathering around their Visual Control Board. Today, David, the Audit Manager, is present. He tries to attend these audit team Standups a couple of times a week, at a minimum, so his team gets ready access to him.

Later in the day, the Single Combined Team will come together at a 2:00 Standup to touch base. But now, in the morning, this is just the auditors getting themselves squared away. David wonders for a moment if the client has their own Standups for a similar purpose, and decides this client probably doesn't. They haven't experienced Lean yet, so Standups as a concept are new to them. They're scheduled to begin a Value Stream assessment in about a month, but aside from some early discussions they don't know a lot about Lean. If they did, he muses, they probably would have their own similar meeting.

He reflects that at least they had the presence of mind to replicate part of the Visual Control Board (VCB) down in their office space. At the end of every 2:00 Standup, one of their staff takes a picture of the main VCB, and updates it to a replica taped to a wall in a hallway in HR. "It's a start," he thinks.

It's time to begin.

The purpose of this meeting is to be sure all the known tasks are represented on the Two-Week Panel, and the Work Progress Panel correctly describes the status of each Control Objective. There is an interdependent relationship between the two panels. Where the Work Progress Panel shows fieldwork for a certain Control Objective is falling behind, a sticky note task will get added to the Two-Week Panel to address it. Where the Work Progress Panel indicates everything is done and is awaiting workpaper review, David will add one of his red stickies to the Two-Week Panel as a reminder. He'll give it a due date based on when his team says they need it. No point in getting that workpaper reviewed immediately if what they really need is comments on observations they need to send to the client tomorrow.

Standing next to the Work Progress Panel, Samir starts the discussion by walking the group through the Control Objectives included in this Iteration. He passes quickly over the ones whose Andon is fully colored in. Those are entirely done. Their fieldwork steps are completed and the workpapers reviewed and approved. Those Control Objectives didn't generate any observations. He moves on to those whose Andons still have white space. Those aren't complete.

He points out three where the fieldwork portion of the Andon is only partially colored in. He turns to Julia and asks if she's made any more progress on these. She has. She gets up and colors two of them in further.

She remarks that the remaining one is giving her trouble. The analysis of the data she wanted to do isn't working properly. It might be she's messing up the pivot table, or it might be that she's thinking about the analysis wrong.

Samir glances over to the Two-Week Panel to see if there is a sticky related to getting this Control Objective completed. There isn't one specific to the data analysis issue, but there is a sticky that denotes Julia is working on this Control Objective this week and intends to complete it by end-of-day Thursday. He decides that's enough for now. He tells Julia that if it continues to be a problem and will affect her Thursday deadline to let him know. He doesn't want to post too many minor stickies on the VCB. She's got a couple of things she can try which should resolve the issue quickly. If those don't work, she can get help from Samir. At tomorrow's team Standup, he'll have an opportunity to ask whether it sorted itself out.

Samir notes where the Andons on several Control Objectives are marked to indicate that their observations have been written and shared with the client, but their facts haven't been agreed. He looks over at the Two-Week Panel to see when the meeting will occur with the clients to go over these observations. He panics for a second when he doesn't see it scheduled in the next two weeks. But then he peeks at the >2 Week Section and sees a sticky there that says, *"Hold observation meeting with clients for Iteration B."*

The >2 Weeks Section ("look forward" section) contains tasks that need to occur, but are further than two weeks out. He relaxes for a moment, but then recalls that it is often difficult to get time with the Business Owner and Governance Layer Owner together. Routinely, their schedules are fully booked for at least two weeks. Yikes!

To have any chance of holding that observation meeting, he probably should have started scheduling it yesterday or the day before. He quickly writes a sticky and puts it on today's column to remind him to get that meeting scheduled. He writes, *"Schedule Obs Meeting, - Iter. B"* and includes the initials of all the clients who need to attend. Taking a breath, he confirms his initial panic when he glances at the Master Calendar Panel and sees that three weeks from now, both the Governance Layer Owner and Business Owner have several conflicts. Whew. Good catch! Any longer, and scheduling that important meeting this month would have been nearly impossible.

Samir relaxes a bit. It still might be difficult to navigate the Governance Layer Owner's and Business Owner's schedules, but he can get help later today at the team Standup. The Single Combined Team will probably have some good ideas how to arrange the Governance Layer Owner's and Business Owner's schedules to make that meeting possible.

Samir takes the group back through the last Iteration. There are a couple of Andons with tiny slivers un-colored; next to them are tiny checkmarks. These indicate that all the fieldwork for those Control Objectives is done, and they'd be entirely complete except the workpapers haven't been finalized. The checkmarks indicate the number of times they've been reviewed and comments given by David, the Audit Manager.

With some chagrin, Samir offers to the group that making the corrections David requested is taking longer than it should. However, he's pleased to point out that he's posted a sticky on the Two-Week Panel that demonstrates he has a plan for getting them done.

David catches himself being a little irritated. He doesn't like having work from previous Iterations carrying forward into the next. But he knows it happens and at least it's visible. Prior to using this system, he recalls, it probably wouldn't be until the end of the audit that he'd notice the workpaper comments had not been addressed. By then, Samir would barely remember the subject, and any value the refinements could have had would have long since passed.

The audit team Standup continues for about another 30 minutes, working the board, making sure tasks are identified and people are coordinated. David gets several more *"review and comment…"* stickies assigned to him. And he's able to color in a few more.

He waits to do so in public at the afternoon Single Combined Team Standup. He tells himself that he's modeling good behavior when he colors in stickies in front of the group, but he really knows it's a better serotonin rush when there is an audience. He knows he's a ham.

Visual Management Principles

The power of Visual Management rests on three key principles:

1. Make waste visible so it can be attacked and eliminated.
2. A coordinated team with a shared understanding of the task is unstoppable.
3. When it's visual, it's harder to ignore.

A good friend, David Winter, who leads the Continuous Improvement team for the West's most extensive water utility, once said, "The greatest sin any manager can commit is to walk past a Visual Control Board that is blinking red and fail to put Countermeasures in place."

It is perhaps a greater sin, though, to have no Visual Control Board in the first place to walk past.

As we discussed in the opening section, when we did an analysis of our cycle time, we found that only about 33% of the elapsed time of an audit was value-added fieldwork. Most of the rest was wait time. Rather than remain idle during this time, we'd shift our attention to something else. This made us feel good. We felt active and utilized.

But we ignored the cost in time required to reacquaint ourselves with the work when the waiting was over and we could perform the next step. It got really bad when, on one audit, the clients came to us and asked for three months to react to the observations we'd sent them. According to them, there was an incredibly urgent priority that would mean they needed to set aside the audit for a bit.

Foolishly, we agreed and began another audit in the meantime. We patted ourselves on the back for being efficient.

Three months stretched into five, and by the time we all returned to the table, we'd forgotten what we knew and they'd forgotten what they'd agreed to previously. We were forced to set aside the audit to which we'd shifted, so that we could relearn the information we used to know.

It was a mess. Paradoxically, as we relearned the facts about the delayed audit, we were fast forgetting the facts of the one we'd picked up and then set aside. The cycle was repeating itself.

Worse, it all happened invisibly – through emails, hallway conversations, and undocumented meetings. We didn't realize what we were doing to ourselves. In fact, we probably felt a bit heroic for juggling so many balls at once. We woke up nine months later, with no resolution and a far lower quality understanding of the material.

This could never happen again. Wait time and rework had to become visible.

FYA vs. FYI

We are all familiar with the initials FYI: **For Your Information**. All kinds of things cross our desks that are FYI. And much of what passes erroneously for Visual Management is just that. Prior to my former organization's Lean journey, it was common to find charts and graphs on walls that showed number of accidents or number of service calls responded to. These were declarations of fact. But they didn't help drive action.

Conversely, FYA means **For Your Action**. It's a very different thing. The chief difference between the two is an indicator that demonstrates quickly and decisively whether the statements of fact are where they should be.

Near my house on a winding road in Colorado is a digital speedometer sign, erected to show drivers how fast they are going. It's the sort of device that police sometimes tow into place. However, this one is permanent. It's even made of sculpted wrought iron to help it fit aesthetically with the community. I rolled by that sign a hundred times and hit my brake each time, before I realized the problem.

The problem is that nowhere on that road is there a speed limit sign telling me the legally acceptable speed. The sign provides FYI, not FYA. From that fairly expensive, solar powered sign I only received a single data point and I need at least two.

Perhaps it did its job on one level, because I always slowed down – briefly. But I had no way of telling whether I was already under the speed limit. So, just as quickly I resumed my former speed after passing.

As you consider all the ways you might employ Visual Management in your audit work, it's crucial to keep in mind the difference between FYI and FYA. Always set a control limit or target that tells you whether you are in or out of tolerance, spec, or control.

It isn't as easy as it might seem to ward off FYI. FYI sneaks up on us. This is because every one of us, when provided with a fact or number (perhaps number of injuries in the workplace) immediately assigns our own acceptable tolerance. With workplace injuries, for example, we automatically assign a tolerance level of zero. We never want anyone to ever be injured. Then we assume everyone else has the same tolerance level. Most of us set such a tolerance within about 10 seconds of hearing the original injury metric, and therefore we never notice that it really never was officially established – at least not to drive action. The missing risk tolerance decision isn't visible because we made it internally in a flash. It becomes an implied tolerance level.

Why is that bad?

It's bad for two reasons. First, we don't actually have an articulated shared understanding of the target state. Without that, any solution that seems to generate fewer injuries will be good enough. And we'll all feel good about having made a move in the right direction. But if we really mean zero injuries, and we have a shared agreement around that target, then we have a far greater likelihood of installing proper Countermeasures (some of which might even be draconian and/or expensive) to get us to zero.

The second reason is more insidious. When we take an FYI approach, where we assume everyone else has the same tolerance level that we internally assigned, in my experience, we're actually more likely to also assume someone else is working on it. In our example, since "everyone knows" that we don't want injuries, it seems reasonable that everyone will be doing their best to avoid them. Concern about the subject won't translate into action at all. When the email with injury statistics for last month arrives, you might grimace and feel some concern, but you won't take real action.

You'll brake for a moment, then resume your previous speed.

Five-Panel Visual Control Board

The visual management system we created for Active Auditing involves five panels. They are interdependent, but each serves a different purpose. The full Visual Control Board (VCB) has spots for the following:

1. Work Progress Panel
2. Two-Week Panel
3. Master Calendar Panel
4. Shared Agreements Panel
5. Hearts & Minds Panel

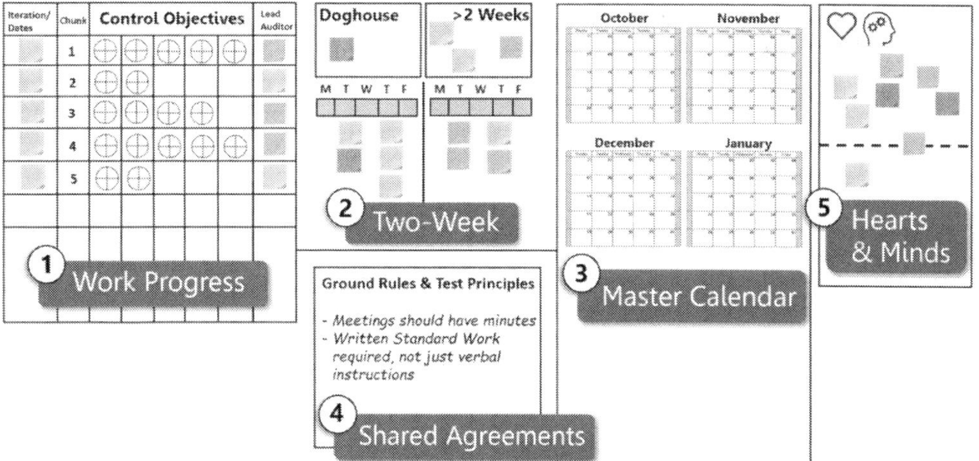

Panel 1 – Work Progress

The Work Progress Panel (WPP), sometimes called the Control Objectives Panel, contains the complete audit program laid out in a Control Objective-based architecture. It describes the work to be done and tracks its progress.

Each Control Objective occupies a small box on the WPP. The boxes are grouped by subject area, which often is synonymous with Iteration, but not always. Their order doesn't matter; the first row of Control Objectives on the WPP might be worked in the last Iteration. Assigning groups of Control Objectives to specific Iterations is a flexible process, so we use sticky notes to mark the assigned time-boxed dates. Changing our minds about which Iteration will work on them is therefore a simple matter of rearranging stickies.

Panel 1 – Work Progress

	Iteration Dates	Subject Area	Control Objectives					Lead Auditor
Iteration A –	1/7-1/18	1	Control Objective Text goes here	Control Objective Text goes here	Control Objective Text goes here	Control Objective Text goes here	Control Objective Text goes here	Samir
Iteration D –	2/25-3/12	2	Control Objective Text goes here	Control Objective Text goes here				Samir
Iteration B –	1/21-2/8	3	Control Objective Text goes here	Control Objective Text goes here	Control Objective Text goes here	Control Objective Text goes here		Sara
Iteration C –	2/11-2/22	4	Control Objective Text goes here	Control Objective Text goes here	Control Objective Text goes here	Control Objective Text goes here	Control Objective Text goes here	Samir
Iteration D –	2/25-3/12	5	Control Objective Text goes here	Control Objective Text goes here				Julia

In the most expansive version of this Panel, and the easiest to use, the Control Objective boxes are sized to accommodate a common sticky note, or about 3"x3" square. This is convenient, but not required. The same process can be accomplished with a white board and markers, or smaller stickies. On-the-road audits might find it more convenient to use 11"x17" sheets or flip-chart-sized paper.

The mechanics aren't as important as the activity.

Components of WPP

Your WPP should have the following components:

- All Control Objectives – including a short description and an Andon
- Column for Assigned Iteration – including time-boxed dates on sticky notes
- Lead Auditor – denotes who is leading or primarily responsible for the work of that Iteration; might always be the Audit Owner, depending on the size of audit and team

Beyond these three components, feel free to write or post whatever else you wish on your WPP. For example, if keeping track of workpaper comments is challenging, use additional detail on the WPP to show which Control Objectives are pending comments.

If your audit involves data requests requiring long lead times, create an indicator on the WPP that shows you instantly which Control Objectives have had the requests made, whether they were understood by the client, and whether they have been received.

If during your post-Iteration reassessment, the team decides to withdraw a Control Objective from fieldwork, place a white sticky over it, so you can easily see which areas are no longer being worked.

As an additional example, keeping track of large numbers of observations is often challenging. Using Visual Management to assist, number the observations, and mark the observation number on the WPP next to the Control Objective it regards. Doing so helps the team talk about the observation more easily at Standups, and tracking progress becomes a team exercise.

As each observation sheet is sent to the client for their reaction, scribble over the observation number on the WPP with a pink highlighter. This instantly tells everyone which observations the client has received and which are still under development. If an Iteration is coming to an end, and several observation numbers remain un-highlighted on the WPP, the team can see easily that they need to either be expedited or reconsidered and removed.

Each audit has different needs, and the WPP should evolve to assist. It should make it easy to know whether the audit is progressing on schedule, what areas are lagging behind, and where Countermeasures should best be applied.

Use the system flexibly and in ways that make sense – always erring on the side of increased visibility.

Andons

An Andon in the Active Auditing system is a quadrisected circle that gets colored in with black marker as progress is achieved. Each sliver or slice has meaning. In the broadest terms, filling in ¼ of an Andon indicates one-quarter of the work is completed.

For example, on a task sticky, an Andon simply has four quadrants, each roughly equivalent to 25% completion.

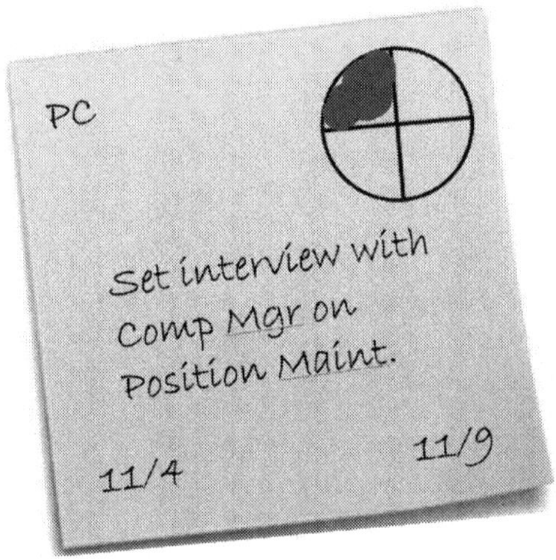

However, for the Work Progress Panel we use an Andon with greater granularity. These Andons serve to demonstrate the progress of each Control Objective, including audit testing, formalization of observations, responses to observations, and implementation of mitigating action plans.

The way our team approached the "real estate" on the Andons is to use two quarters for the audit team's work (completion of testing and review thereof, and delivery of observations and obtaining agreement thereon) and two quarters for the client team's work (creating and delivering mitigating action plans, and carrying out those action plans).

When fieldwork steps for a Control Objective are finished, most of a quarter piece of "the pie" gets filled in by the auditor most responsible for the work. A small sliver remains unfilled until the Audit Oversight reviews the associated workpapers and approves them.

Example: Work Progress Panel (HR Audit)

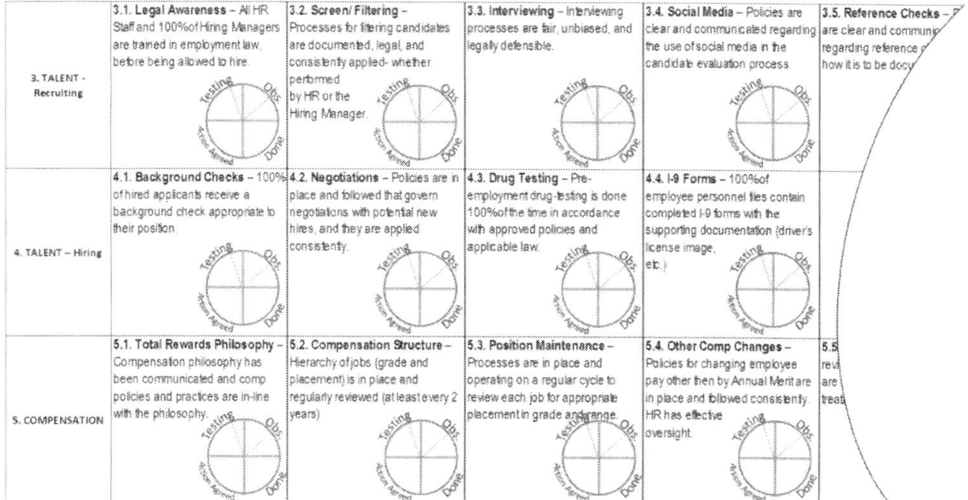

When any observations resulting from the fieldwork are written and ready to be shared with the clients, part of the next ¼ is be colored in. The remainder of that quarter gets colored in when those observations are agreed as to their facts with the client. At this point, the entire top half of the Andon is colored black. This means the auditor's portion of the work is done. The bottom half of the Andon belongs to the client. When the client has determined a mitigating action plan for the associated observations, they may color in the next quarter. When the client has completed the action plan, they may color in the final quarter.

At the point all the top halves are colored black, it becomes possible to peel the WPP off the wall and reposition it in the Business Owner's or Governance Layer Owner's office. They can use it to visually keep track of their mitigation progress.

WPP Andon Key

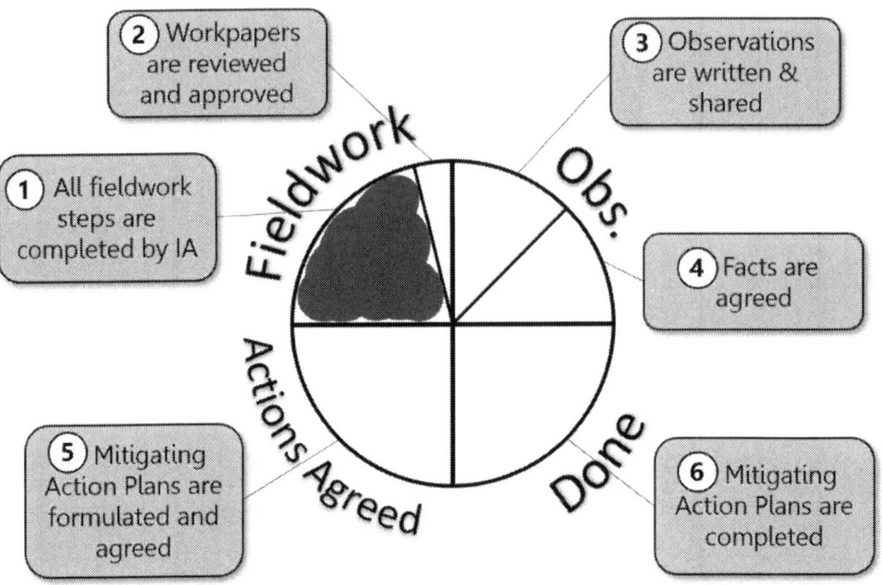

WPP Setup

Setting up the WPP isn't difficult, particularly if you've structured your audit program around Control Objectives or something similar. We recommend structuring around Control Objectives, both because there will be fewer Control Objectives than fieldwork steps, which makes them more manageable, and because the Control Objectives are less likely to change than any single fieldwork step.

When you can create what Lean refers to as an Obeya or "war room" for the audit, we recommend producing your WPP on a large format printer or plotter. Perhaps it's a wall in Internal Audit's suite or a space in the client's area. It's easier for the Single Combined Team to circle up around a 3'x4' sheet than a smaller one. However, big paper is not always practical, especially for traveling auditors. So do the best you can. A whiteboard in a conference room for a one-week traveling audit works just as well.

If you have auditors in multiple places, perhaps thousands of miles apart, we recommend passing cellphone pictures back and forth and maintaining WPPs in each location. This sounds time consuming and tedious, but the payoff in terms of team understanding of progress is more than worth it.

Technologizing the VCB

Whenever I discuss setting up a VCB, someone usually suggests automating it – putting it on SharePoint or Workfront. Folks have even approached me to build Active Auditing software.

The Lean wizards at Toyota and I both recommend you resist the temptation.

Lean teaches that going to look at a computer screen is usually an activity for a single person in isolation. It's solitary and doesn't advance team understanding. It's a wasted opportunity.

Don't get me wrong, I can certainly imagine digital dashboards such as you might see in the movies *Star Trek* or *Minority Report* lining the walls of an Internal Audit Obeya. It would be really nifty to convert our $50 home improvement store whiteboards into gorgeous, and expensive, digital screens. With such digitalization, we could beam the information across the globe instantly, and stop buying crates of sticky notes.

But aside from the obvious expense, we'd lose the instant flexibility that comes from manual processes. If we wanted to add a notation on the WPP to track something new just for this audit, we'd need to submit a software request. It would take time. And the tools would be dictating the work, rather than the other way around.

Lean and the Toyota Way teach only employing reliable, thoroughly tested technology that serves your people and processes. Most automation today doesn't meet these requirements. One day, we'll no doubt conduct audits using digital VCBs where the sticky notes are voice-activated and the screens run floor to ceiling. I'd certainly enjoy leading Standups in such a fancy Obeya, with the Single Combined Team joining in from anywhere in the world.

I'm told Toyota is doing some of this today, putting up digital VCBs where they can be seen by the entire team, as technology becomes cheaper and easier to modify. Sadly, we expect it will be some time before serious technologizing of Active Auditing makes sense in most internal audit shops.

Until software and automation can enhance the collaborative experience, we strongly recommend sticking with stickies.

Panel 2 – Two-Week

The Two-Week Panel comes in three parts:

1. Daily Board
2. >2 Weeks Section
3. Doghouse

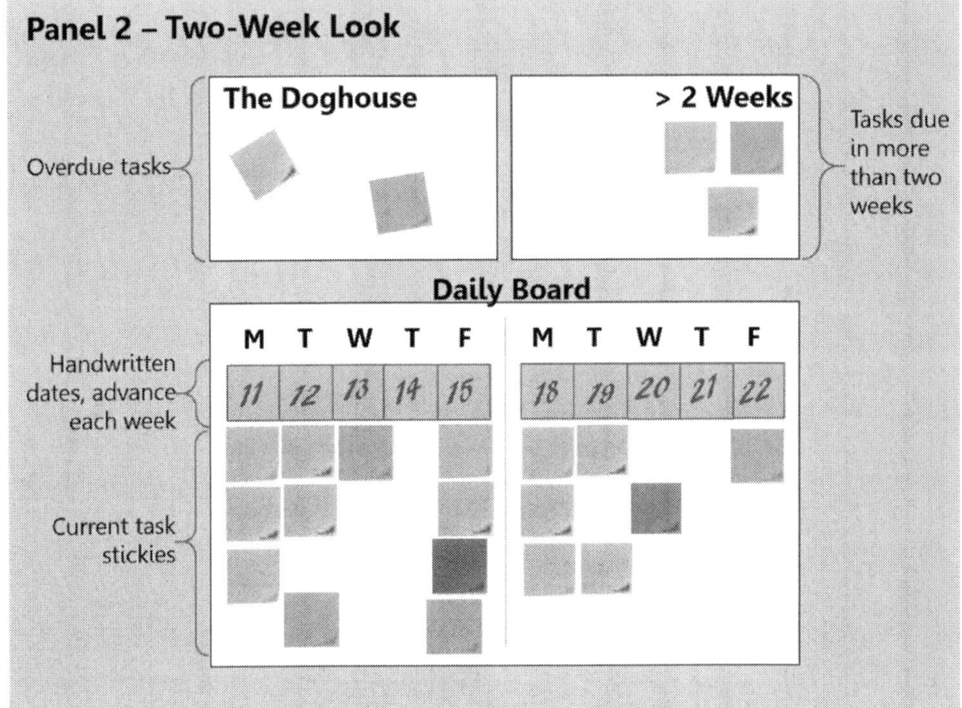

Daily Board

The Daily Board contains columns for each day of the next two weeks. It's where the "planning" stops and the "doing" gets tracked. The Daily Board is a living machine for communicating about work. On it you'll place the important tasks for the audit that need to occur over the coming 10 business days.

At the end of each week, usually Friday afternoon when everyone is worn out anyhow, the team takes time to advance the Two-Week Panel by one week. Advancing means shifting the dates and their associated tasks one week to the left. Any task stickies that didn't get done either get reassigned to a day in the next week or shifted to the Doghouse. Any tasks from the

>2 Weeks Section that are now due within the upcoming two weeks are placed under the appropriate date. And the cycle of work begins again.

Anatomy of a Sticky

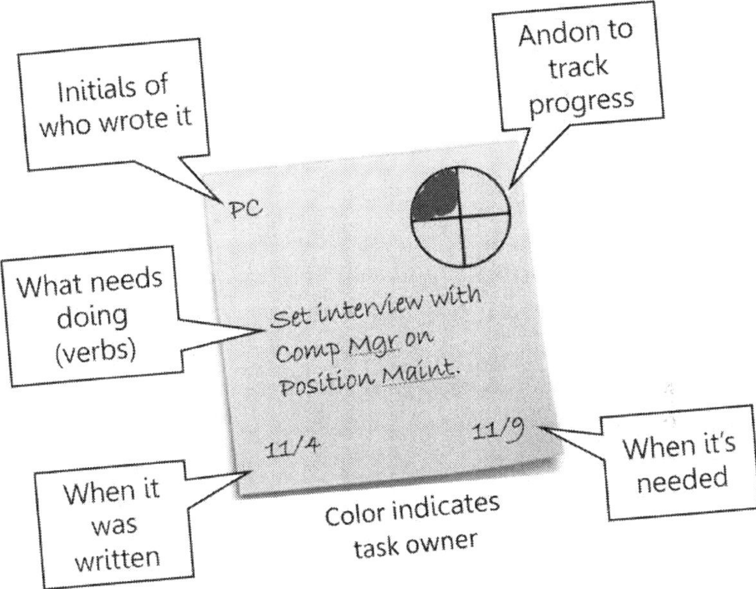

Sticky Etiquette – At the beginning of the audit, each member of the Single Combined Team chooses a sticky color to be their own. Yes, this means having a huge number of sticky color options available, from hot pink to seafoam. If this isn't practical, or if a team member is color blind, you can just use one or two colors with team member initials in the corner. However, colors make Visual Management significantly easier.

The act of a team member choosing their color also applies a helpful tinge of ownership. It's like putting on the team jersey or putting your hand in on a stack of hands right before a team goes on the field for the game. It says, "Well, if I went so far as to pick a color, maybe I'm really part of this team. My participation is visible to all."

Have each team member write their name on a sticky of their color and find a spot off to the side of the Two-Week Panel to display them. Having a color-key reminds everyone who is on the roster of this team and it is a quick mnemonic for when you forget who has dark green, for instance.

As tasks are identified, write a shorthand description on a task sticky and place it under the date it is due. Generally, ownership is increased if the person responsible writes it for themselves. However, that's not always practical. Anytime a task sticky is written by someone other than the owner, it becomes the duty of the writer to inform the owner. Often, it can be as simple as taking a cellphone pic of the sticky and sending it to the owner of the task.

Similarly, it's often a useful upward management technique for the Audit Owner to prepare task stickies for the Chief Audit Executive or Audit Oversight role to let them know when action is needed. For example, if workpapers are ready for review, the Audit Owner might write a sticky in the Audit Oversight's color and place it on the day the review is needed.

Stickies should have action verbs in their descriptions, not just subjects or nouns. *"View hiring manager training video"* is preferred over *"Training Video."* *"Set Interview with Greg on data sample"* is better than *"Data Sample - Greg."* You'll be surprised by the difference in team member behavior if you enforce action verbs on stickies.

What's on a task sticky? – A task sticky has five data elements, in addition to its color, described in the "Anatomy of a Sticky" diagram. Remember, the color defines who owns the task.

What merits a task sticky? – The Two-Week Panel is a communications tool more than it's a work management engine. It's not Microsoft Project or Workfront. It isn't practical to put every action that will occur on a sticky. Instead, we want tasks on the Panel that need to be understood and/or monitored by other members of the Single Combined Team.

We suggest the following guidelines:

- If it is reasonably likely the task will need assistance from someone else… it should be a sticky.
- If it marks an important milestone, such as completion of a significant collection of fieldwork steps… it should be a sticky.
- If it describes either setting or holding a meeting/interview… it should be a sticky.
- If one team member needs other team members to be aware of the task… it should be a sticky.

- If it helps the Audit Oversight or Chief Audit Executive understand the status of the audit… it should be a sticky.

What shouldn't be a sticky? Generally, we recommend erring on the side of putting tasks on stickies until you've got a good sense of what works for the team. Tasks that solely involve one team member probably shouldn't be stickies. Tasks that happen as fast as the sticky can be written and closed probably don't need to be stickies. Use more stickies than you probably expect. Stickies are cheap. A screwed up audit is expensive.

Can stickies be moved? – Yes, you may shift stickies around on the Panel. Active Auditing is flexible. Change your plan as needed. You won't lose much, since the original target date is a component of the sticky.

However, DO NOT rearrange stickies without the task owner's involvement. It's a mutual purpose sin to shift a deadline without the task owner knowing, even if it's a shift to a later date. If necessary, establish a Shared Ground Rule that only the Audit Owner has the right to move stickies and they promise to always alert and obtain the concurrence of the task owner if it becomes necessary.

I'm often asked when should a sticky be moved versus when should it go in the Doghouse. The answer is, "It depends."

Mostly the guidance I give relates to the firmness of the deadline. If not accomplishing the task puts completion of the Iteration in jeopardy, it should go to the Doghouse. If the original deadline was flexible, then move it to a better target date. Be aware, though, that the first move might be to a new date, while subsequent moves may be to the Doghouse, because there is no longer slack available in the schedule.

>2 Weeks Section

The >2 Weeks Section is sometimes called the "Look Forward" area. In this section, place any task stickies you know you will need to do, but which aren't needed in the next 10 business days. This is a parking lot for tasks.

As the audit progresses and you advance the Daily Board (usually each Friday), examine the >2 Week Section to see if any parked task stickies have target dates in the upcoming ten business days. Pull those down and place them on the date they are needed.

We recommend deliberately reviewing the >2 Weeks Section at each

Standup. Frequently, the team will realize that something that is set to occur three weeks from now needs preparatory attention now. Perhaps a meeting that is needed in three weeks needs to be scheduled tomorrow. Account for those by leaving the task sticky related to holding the meeting in the >2 Weeks Section and creating a separate task sticky related to scheduling the meeting. Place the scheduling sticky in tomorrow's column on the Daily Board.

What goes in the >2 Weeks Section? – It's sometimes hard to know how far out to look in the future. After all, it could be argued that you should fill this space with every task for their entire audit. Doing so, however, would be counter to Iterative Execution. It would be Waterfall thinking and would be the sticky note equivalent of a full project schedule. Don't do it.

Instead, capture what you know needs to occur for this Iteration only and any pre-work necessary for future Iterations, but don't go overboard. Anticipate and plan, but don't overdo it. A lot of it will change. Piles of task stickies in the >2 Weeks Section verges on committing the Lean Waste of "inventory" and, because change is likely, it also represents "overproduction" and "defects & rework."

The Doghouse

This section is cordoned off for the task stickies that, by their delinquency, are putting timely completion of the Iteration, or the entire audit, at risk.

So, at the end of each week when you are advancing the WPP, locate any task stickies that are uncompleted and past their target dates. If they can't be assigned to a new target date without jeopardizing the Iteration schedule, they belong in the Doghouse.

During Standups, spend a fair amount of time on any task stickies that appear here. Take whatever steps are necessary to clear Doghouse stickies. Elevate them to the Business Owner or Governance Layer Owner, if necessary. If the task owner of a Doghouse sticky isn't showing up to Standups, take a picture and email it to them and their boss.

A sticky in the Doghouse is a blinking red light on a control board. It's the check engine light on your car's dashboard. Countermeasures are necessary.

Sticky stack or trophy wall? – As tasks are completed, and team members have enjoyed filling in their Andons, you have a choice of what to do with them. We recommend one of two approaches – a sticky stack or a trophy wall.

A sticky stack is simply an ever-growing pile of stickies adjacent to the VCB. Watching the stack grow is a visual reminder of how much work the Single Combined Team has done together. It helps build esprit de corps.

A trophy wall, on the other hand, celebrates the contributions of specific members of the team. A trophy wall is a designated portion of the VCB where completed stickies are placed for the world to see. As team members complete their tasks, with fanfare they fill in their Andons and dramatically peel and smack them somewhere on the trophy wall.

Even the trophy wall can be done several different ways, which have different potential behavioral effects. One method makes trophies only out of stickies that represent significant effort. The other method celebrates how many completed stickies each team member has completed, which becomes visible as the proportion of the trophy wall covered by a given color increases over time. Team members can enjoy showing off that they've got the most stickies in their color on the trophy wall.

Often it's a good idea for the auditors to leave the trophy wall for the clients and just keep their own sticky stack off to the side, but it doesn't really matter. It's just one more way to create mutual purpose. It helps make accomplishing things as a team fun.

Panel 3 – Master Calendar

I'd like to make the concept of a Master Calendar difficult, but I can't.

And even while the concept is simple, and the benefits considerable, prior to creating the Active Auditing approach, I'd never seen it done.

The Master Calendar is a Visual Management tool to track team member availability and to show important milestones.

Through my career, this sort of thing was usually covered in the entrance meeting with a request to the clients by the auditor-in-charge to let us know when anyone will be on vacation. Habitually, that request was met with silence in the meeting and surprises later.

To build the Master Calendar Panel, start by printing monthly calendars for each month the audit will take place. We recommend adding one more calendar than you think you need so you can visualize the consequences of not completing on time. 11"x17" paper for each month is sufficient, but it's even better if you can get the days to be close to the size of a standard 3"x3" sticky. Cut off the weekends, unless you expect to work on those days.

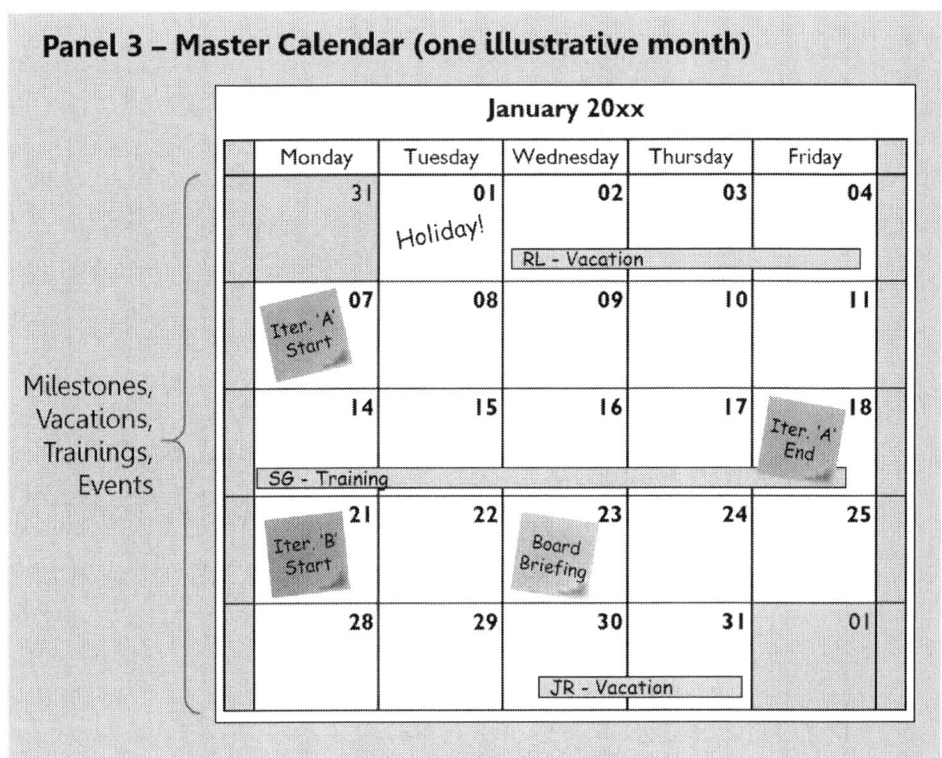

For short audits, measured in days or weeks, we recommend printing and posting at least a full month and maybe two. You'll want to show all the Iterations as well as the reporting phase. Make sure you mark dates for the closing celebration and Retrospective.

After you've taped the calendars to your VCB, ask each team member to mark any days they expect to be unavailable for at least half a day. You may also ask team members to indicate days or weeks when their team is virtually unavailable for audit matters due to urgent priorities (e.g., the financial reporting team is unavailable for the first three business days of each fiscal month due to a tight monthly close process).

A technique that works well is to use thin 3/8" masking tape laid across each unavailable day. Masking tape works because you can write the team member's initials and nature of the outage on it, and peel it later if things change. How you do it doesn't matter. Demonstrating you really care about this info, collecting it, and keeping it current is what's important.

Next, with stickies, mark the beginning and ending dates of each Iteration. We enjoy using cheerful cloud-shaped stickies, but it can be done any way you like.

At each Standup, ask the team to re-verify that their information remains accurate. If you have important team members who don't regularly show up for Standup (not preferred, but not uncommon), the Audit Owner should write themselves a sticky periodically to request those team members stop by and update their Master Calendar information. Pay particular attention to the Chief Audit Executive and Governance Layer Owner. Long periods where the Chief Audit Executive and Governance Layer Owner don't review their information on the Master Calendar can spell trouble.

On one audit, we were surprised when the Administrative Assistant to the Governance Layer Owner attended her first Standup and remarked that his boss would shortly be in Europe for nearly a month. The Governance Layer Owner hadn't been to Standup in a while, and the upcoming absence was never marked on the Master Calendar. The news disrupted the audit.

Nonetheless, at least we received some notice. In a traditional audit, we'd likely first find this out when trying to schedule a meeting during her vacation. As disruptive as it was, we were able to navigate the situation using the Master Calendar.

If you anticipate having issues with attendance at Standups, create a chart with each team member's name down the left side and columns for each day of the audit across the top. At the end of each Standup, take attendance. Mark those present with a green dot and those absent with red. Tape this chart where members of the Single Combined Team will see it at each Standup. It helps demonstrate you care who shows up, and gives you the data to foresee when absenteeism will cause problems later.

Panel 4 – Shared Agreements

Two types of things go on the Shared Agreements Panel.

Shared Ground Rules are the first. If, when you followed Essential #3 at the beginning of the audit, you took the time to type up Shared Ground Rules, then tape a copy to the Shared Agreements Panel. If there are just a handful, write them using whiteboard marker. The Shared Agreements Panel is in the center of the VCB, so it is always front and center. Put on it things that will help drive healthy interactions between the members of the Single Combined Team.

Testing Principles are the second. Often it's useful to post how the auditors will be "keeping score." Testing Principles often regard what constitutes a sufficient fieldwork test across a number of tests. This list usually evolves through the audit. Examples of Testing Principles include:

- If it wasn't written down, we can't assume it was done.
- Some kind of mark (initials, etc.) is required to validate a document was reviewed by management.
- Meeting minutes are required to accept that something was discussed.
- Written procedures are required, not just verbal instructions or a long-held understanding.

These are similar to Shared Ground Rules, but much more tactical. Posting them is useful because it helps everyone know the rules. They help make the audit feel less arbitrary. When everyone understands, it's much less likely for participants to feel like they are being picked on. You may not have many Testing Principles, but leave a space for them. Sometimes you'll get into an argument with your clients and a healthy way of diffusing the energy can be to establish a mutually agreed Testing Principle.

Panel 5 – Hearts & Minds

The Hearts & Minds Panel is arguably the most powerful tool in Active Auditing. It's the tool auditors use to show they are serious about energetically collaborating. It's also the panel that generates the most "whoa, wait a minute… I can't do that" reactions from audit managers when I explain it.

It can be scary. It's messy human stuff. You can't control it.

But you need to do it if you are going to succeed at Active Auditing.

Hearts & Minds deals with how people involved with the audit are feeling, what they're afraid of, and their hopes and anticipations when it comes to the audit. As we discussed in Pillar One: Energetic Collaboration, the auditors are in the power position. If we're going to really get past that and become human with each other, we've got to demonstrate that we care about how we make the clients feel. This is one way we do that.

Hearts & Minds is borrowed from Lean, which is a change-making process. Change is hard on people, and Lean recognizes that.

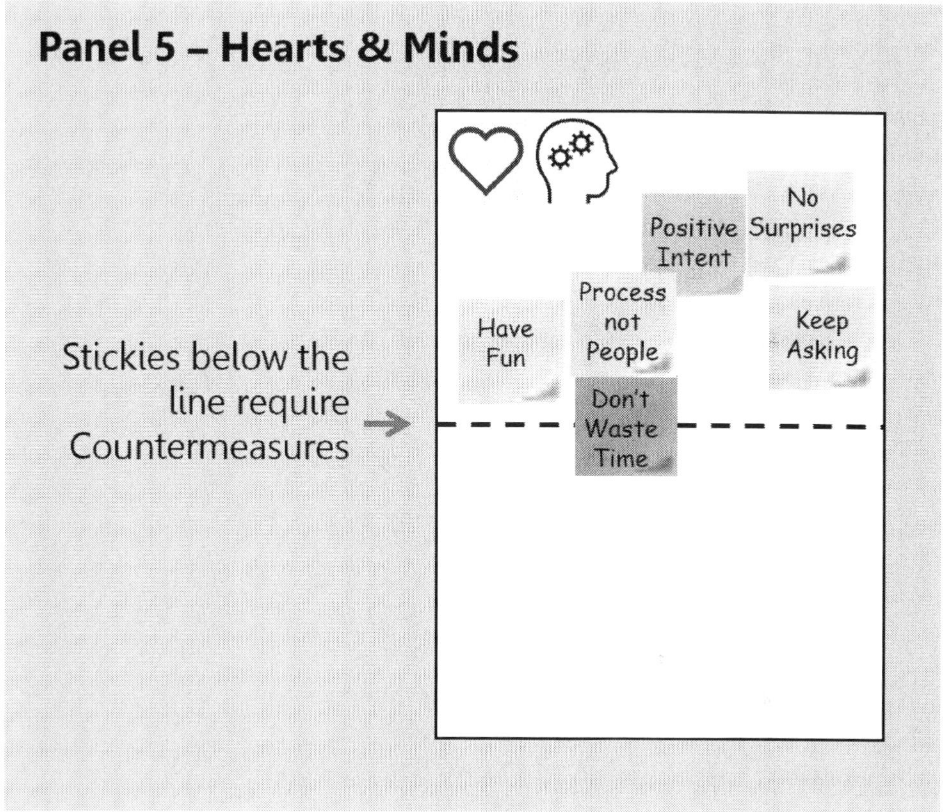

As a grad student at Colorado State University, I enjoyed a class on organizational change management. The most valuable thing I learned in that course wasn't from the textbook or the professor. It came from a whitehaired, blue-collar Water Treatment Technician who the professor invited to speak to the class. Little did I know that 20 years later I would work for a water utility undergoing substantial change as well.

This fellow, whose name I'll never recall, but who looked a lot like the actor Morgan Freeman and had the same gravitas, came to speak about a huge change that had happened to him and how he and his colleagues dealt with it. He had worked for decades at a water treatment facility located along the Poudre River, high up in Poudre Canyon west of Fort Collins, Colorado. Poudre Canyon is a world class trout stream and, except for Highway 14 that runs alongside it, a stunning stretch of western American river. Rafting companies make a living guiding tourists down this river from early spring through the end of summer. It's a marvel.

It seemed the treatment facility in which he'd spent most of his career was only marginally newer than the canyon itself. It dated to 1905. For those who aren't native to the West, that means it dated to the "cowboy days." That's old for the western U.S.

For nearly 30 years, he'd loved working there. He loved the history and the feeling of connection to the canyon. He talked about loving the sounds of the red-throated hummingbirds zooming around just outside the plant's front door. However, in 1987 it closed in favor of a newer facility, no longer in the canyon, closer to the city and located on the plains. He was devastated. The professor, as I recall, had worked with the water utility to soften the blow for the workers. That's how she knew him. And the result of her work evidently was a much more interactive and positive change than would have typically occurred.

This water treatment plant technician told the assembled class of MBA students, who were likely to make twice his salary they day they graduated, that he'd really appreciated that the utility had cared how he felt and asked him the best ways to make the transition. He was nearly in tears as he talked about the change. I recall one phrase vividly, which tells you why Active Auditing employs the Hearts & Minds Panel.

He said, "People don't mind change. Heck, they're always buying the newest of everything – computers, TVs, or whatever." In his down-to-earth manner, he went on to say, "What people mind is <u>being</u> changed. That... they'll go to war against."

It was one of the most valuable things I heard in my entire MBA program, and as far as I know he taught it to me for free.

If we assume he was correct, then we are in the right frame of mind to tackle the Hearts & Minds Panel. As a tool, it isn't difficult. However, doing it properly means you have to be sublimely human, and that can be difficult for auditors.

Here's how it's done.

At a Standup early in the audit, when essentially the entire Single

Combined Team is present, the leader of the Standup says something like the following:

"OK, team, one of the things that sets our audit approach apart from how audits are normally done is that we devote a big chunk of our Visual Control Board to capturing what's on everyone's mind and how they are feeling. Caring about each other through this process is part of how we become a team. It's a technique that some of the biggest companies in the world use to make them more effective, and I think we're worth it."

Pause for a moment to let the introduction settle in. Then continue.

"Everyone take a stack of stickies, doesn't have to be your color. In fact, it's probably better if it isn't. I'd like you to write on the sticky something you'd like to be sure happens in this audit. Or something you are worried about. If you have a ground rule you'd like to be sure gets talked about, write it down and put it up there. You are free to put whatever matters to you."

Pass around stickies and markers. It's often helpful for the auditors to start since they are likely to understand this panel better than the clients. The Standup leader might write something like "No Surprises" and post it on the panel, while explaining, *"Right now I'm going to put this pretty close to the line. If we as a Single Combined Team think we are doing well at making sure we don't surprise each other – and that's true of both the auditors and the clients, maybe we'll decide to move it up a few inches at a future Standup. If we aren't doing so well, we'll be honest with ourselves and move it down, maybe below the line."*

For Single Combined Teams who haven't experienced Active Auditing before, there will be some long pauses during this phase. Clients don't easily trust auditors. Resist the urge to fill those spaces with speech. Let the clients warm to the process in their own time.

It's often useful, in such times, for the auditors to just silently and diligently write a few more statements and, without talking, post them on the Hearts & Minds Panel. Only the most distrustful clients will fail to engage entirely with this process. Remember it might be a well-deserved reputation of IA's that is causing this distrust, so be sensitive to it.

At some point, while this is happening, the Standup leader should then point out that when any sticky falls below the line, the entire team then has an obligation to put in place Countermeasures to ensure it doesn't continue to happen. If the sticky is "No Surprises" and recently the auditors sent over observations merely 5 minutes before a meeting intended to discuss them, perhaps the Countermeasure is a promise to always provide 48 hours of reading time for any observations in the future.

Write agreed Countermeasures on Panel 4 - Shared Agreements, so the team doesn't lose track of them.

This kind of exercise usually behaves like popcorn popping. It starts out with folks having crossed arms and looking at their feet. Then the kernels begin to pop, they pop vigorously for a minute or two, eventually trailing off; with a couple of pops very late. When you reach the point where there aren't many pops, take a few seconds to talk about each sticky.

The Standup leader points to each and asks for clarity. Take no more than 15-20 seconds for each. Sometimes stickies are written in shorthand and the team won't understand them on their face. It's best to take a moment to be sure everyone understands their intent now.

End this part of the Standup, regardless of client contribution, by saying, *"Don't worry, we'll revisit this many times during the audit and you can add stickies whenever you want. Also, feel free to add a sticky when you think of it, even if it's outside of a Standup. If you do, just point it out to me so I know it's there. Thanks, team."*

If you get stonewalled during this process and no clients offer any stickies, don't panic. They may just not be ready. However, keep an eye on it. If after several Standups, the clients have refused to engage, you may have a deep-rooted trust problem. It may be recoverable with some dialog, or it may be so entrenched that full Active Auditing won't work, and you'll be forced to revert to a more traditional approach.

Through the audit, take pictures of your entire VCB and make sure you get the Hearts & Minds Panel "in frame." It makes good material for the Retrospective and the celebration.

FIVE

"It is not necessary to change. Survival is
not mandatory."
– W. Edwards Deming

OBJECTIVES-BASED RISK
ASSESSMENT & PLANNING

The reader is forgiven for assuming that Active Auditing's approach to annual planning is solely to increase its flexibility. It's a reasonable assumption that things will be better if we borrow Agile's iterative concepts to reassess our annual audit plan after each audit, before we start another. That's a relatively simple process and we'd agree. Active Auditing encourages you to constantly and deliberately reassess. Your world has likely changed since the day you got the annual audit plan approved by your board. It may have changed while you were working on this last audit.

So, Active Auditing does advocate that you take a deliberate moment to ask, "What's changed?" at the end of each audit (probably before the end of each audit) and follow that question with, "How should that change affect the next audit?" That's useful, but it doesn't go far enough. It's only part of the story.

How do you build the Active Auditing audit plan in the first place, using Lean and Agile thinking; and how do you do it so it meets Standard 2010 of the *International Standards for the Professional Practice of Internal Auditing*, which says, "The chief audit executive must establish a risk-based plan to determine the priorities of the internal audit activity, consistent with the organization's goals"?

Small Gears

Small gears turn larger gears, which eventually turn the biggest gears. Lean teaches that by improving the effectiveness of dozens/ hundreds/ thousands of small things, the positive effect rolls up to improve the big things. In effect, make a small gear work better at the bottom of the organization and, if the gears are connected properly to the rest of the business engine, the big gears at the top will turn. Perhaps they'll only move one tick to the better, but they'll move. This concept, derived from Lean, recognizes that the interconnectedness of processes goes beyond the workshop or assembly line. It carries into goal setting and strategic planning for the entire organization. And it's a way of looking at risk and annual audit planning that grounds you in the business's objectives.

From an Active Auditing perspective, we apply this thinking to how we conduct risk assessments and how we define an audit universe, which ultimately leads us to defining our annual audit plan.

Strategic Plan-Driven

If we think in terms of small gears turning big gears, we instantly need to know, "What are the big gears?" The clearest answer is that the big gears are the top priorities in the organization's strategic plan.

There are loads of strategic planning formats; almost every organization customizes theirs to meet their specific needs. Nevertheless, they frequently contain the following components:

- Mission, Vision, & Values
- SWOT Analysis (i.e., Strengths, Weaknesses, Opportunities, & Threats)
- Goals & Objectives – Long- and Short-Term
- Key Performance Indicators
- Specific Priorities & Action Plans

- Financial Projections

Not surprisingly, Lean thinking has us focusing on the goals, objectives, and their associated Key Performance Indicators (KPIs). KPIs should be the top-level metrics that define whether an organization is achieving its strategic objectives.

To illustrate, in the utility business (whether it's water, power, cable TV, or sanitation), availability of the utility service is usually paramount. Utility customers, when surveyed, define quality first based on whether the water flows, the cable comes on, or the lights work. Taste of the water, number of channels, and other characteristics typically come second. Consequently, from a strategic planning standpoint, the best utilities usually set and monitor an availability KPI. In the best water utilities, one of the top-level KPIs is usually "customer outage hours." When a water main breaks and homes and businesses are without service, the customer outage calculation tallies up all the people in the area that were without water and multiplies it by the number of minutes until water service was restored. 100 houses times 120 minutes equals 12,000 outage minutes or 200 outage hours.

There are dozens of factors that contribute to why this number goes up or down. For example, if the water utility's monitoring systems don't alert response teams quickly, the metric will increase. If the hand-off between the utility's call center and its field operations is slow; the metric will increase. If shut-off valves in the area haven't received recent preventive maintenance and fail, necessitating finding other shut-off valves further away from the break, the metric will increase as more homes go without water. If trucks aren't positioned properly or crews aren't properly staffed, the metric will increase. The list goes on, but it is largely a knowable list based on understanding the business processes involved.

The best utilities understand and document the contributing business processes to this metric. If they are actively employing Lean thinking, they'll be determining which of those processes have the greatest impact on the customer outage hour KPI and will be actively working to eliminate waste in those processes first. This is how Lean organizations prioritize continuous improvement efforts.

It is also how we recommend Active Audit teams develop their multi-year and annual audit plans. By understanding the contributing business processes, Internal Audit can focus its work on evaluating whether those processes are operating in control. The term "risk" stops being the product of speculative brainstorming, and becomes grounded in the likelihood that these specific contributing processes won't function properly. Discussions of threats and risks are therefore directly connected to objectives. They don't become fanciful "what if" sessions.

Objectives-Based Audit Universe

IIA Practice Advisory 2010-1, describes the audit universe as "a list of all the possible audits that could be performed." Creation of a universe isn't required by professional standards, but it is often a good place to start.

A lot of chief audit executives build their audit universes by:

- Cataloging their organization's departmental structure, portfolio of IT systems, and geographic locations
- Mining existing enterprise risk management work
- Reviewing control self-appraisal (or control self-assessment) data
- Capturing active and planned projects
- Referencing best practices and other industry risk guidance

However, early in our shift from traditional to Active Auditing, we realized that a better way of developing an audit universe, one influenced by Lean thinking, is to structure it around these collections of contributing processes, which feed to an organizational objective and KPI. It's a fairly simple hierarchical map that places the goal, objective, and KPI along the left side and lists the business processes that affect them in the next column. The remaining columns provide data on past audit work and any supporting systems.

To take the objectives-based planning approach a bit further, we began looking at risk differently from what is common in the internal audit profession. Rather than the typical brainstorming of bad things that could happen in a speculative way, we instead ask what business processes must function properly, every day, in order for them to a) not negatively impact the KPI and b) improve that KPI. Those processes most central to meeting the top-line KPIs are then good choices for upcoming audit work.

Objectives-Based Audit Universe Model

Top-Level Goal	Objectives	KPIs	Processes that Must Function Properly to Achieve KPI	Date of Most Recent Audit Work	# of Findings	Criticality to Objective	Criticality to Goal	Supporting IT Systems
Goal A	Objective 1	KPI - A	Business Process 001	--/--/--	N/A	High	High	IT System A
			Business Process 002	--/--/--	4	High	Med	IT System B
			Business Process 003	--/--/--	10	Lo	Lo	IT System C
								IT System D
	Objective 2	KPI - B	Business Process 004	--/--/--	N/A	Med	Med	N/A
			Business Process 005	--/--/--	3	Lo	Med	IT System B
Goal B	Objective 3	KPI - C	Business Process 006	--/--/--	N/A	High	High	IT System E

When we do that audit work, we're not attempting to guess at all the ways it could go wrong – risk brainstorming. Instead, we're evaluating the mechanisms that management has in place to know if it has gone wrong and their capabilities for installing Countermeasures.

Of course, strategic plans come in all shapes and in many levels of quality and seriousness. Lots of organizations publish a strategic plan, but then promptly forget they have one. Or they develop a strategic plan that has no measurements and KPIs; it's simply a directional sign post telling the employees, "Go this way, more or less." When the business isn't driven by it, the plan really doesn't establish the organization's objectives. That's a huge problem, and if it's happening in your organization, you may have your next audit initially scoped.

Proper annual audit planning in organizations without functional strategic plans is significantly more difficult. This is true whether you're talking traditional or Active Auditing.

Absent a guiding set of master objectives, i.e., the big gears, auditors are required to imagine our own priorities and come up with our own view of what's important. That's dangerous.

The best we can usually do is create our own risk matrices, review them with our board, and use them as the basis of annual planning. It's better than nothing, but not by much, when viewed through a Lean lens. It allows us to get on with creating an annual audit plan, but it isn't entirely integrated with the organization's strategy.

SIX

"If everyone is moving forward together,
then success takes care of itself."
– Henry Ford

EPILOGUE

As I've discussed Active Auditing with groups and CAEs, I'm eventually asked whether I think it can work in their organization, or whether there was something special about the ecosystem in which it was developed that made it possible.

Like most genesis events, whether it's the development of the internal combustion engine or the founding of the internet, the right components need to be properly positioned in proximity and time for something new to be born. Undoubtedly, that occurred in our organization and with our team. Had we not experienced the exact right frustrations we did, had we not had multiple years of stable audit data to examine, and had we not had a board and executive team willing to experiment, Active Auditing would have remained an interesting, yet untried, idea.

It seems to me that the trick to exportability for Active Auditing is in the development of mutual purpose. You can certainly employ Visual Management techniques without mutual purpose, but Standups will be uncomfortable and less productive if the classic divide between auditors and the clients continues. And you can certainly break your audits into Iterations, without mutual purpose, but completing all the steps in a time-boxed period, without joint agreement to function as a Single Combined Team will be much more difficult.

So, then, what is the key to developing mutual purpose? We discuss much of this under Pillar One. However, the lynchpin of it all is getting your customer – whether it's the board, the audit committee, or the representatives of the citizenry in a governmental audit context – to recognize that they have an <u>unquestionable right</u> to expect their auditors and their management to function in a unified manner to deliver the audit. Having recognized this right, we then need them to recognize their duty to demand it be so.

Therefore, we recommend that before you sneak out and buy whiteboard sheets to construct your Obeya, and before you develop your VCB and break your audit program into chunks based on Control Objectives, sit down with your governing body and have an honest conversation about their rights and obligations. Share the contents of this book. Acknowledge and accept past mistakes and how high the cliff might be to climb to close the Mutual Purpose Gap. In some organizations it might be too high, at least for the moment. Even so, take a chance and suggest the better way that gets them the assurance services they've paid for in a more efficient and more healthy and constructive way.

There is no reason an internal audit should have a different human dynamic than any other important organizational initiative or project (IT-related or otherwise.)

The next thing we recommend is to start holding Standups. If you can hold them in front of even a makeshift visual control board, all the better. Get folks talking and interacting. In the face of regular contact, it's hard for humans (whether the auditors or the clients) to maintain an "us versus them" dynamic.

And, just as you and your auditors seek to be more vulnerable with your clients, be more human with your customer. Change isn't easy. Lean knows this. Agile knows this. You will need support. Our profession has logged a lot of years behaving in a traditional way. It will take persistence and courage to evolve to something different.

The last thing we encourage you to do is to believe deeply that there can be a better way. When we set out on our Active Auditing journey, I sat down with the second in command of our organization and asked for her backing, which she gave. But she didn't issue an executive order to close the Mutual Purpose Gap. No one can command collaboration. She just provided her support. She listened to those who were confused and complaining and asked them to trust the process. She helped them believe.

Lean teaches that one of the highest hurdles to continuous improvement is that the people involved often think in terms of 15% improvement in the margins; when those who truly believe and let their creativity flow achieve 50% and 75% improvement in throughput, cycle time, defect rates, and whatever. Those who've lived a successful Lean journey know that even the smartest and most capable people can't snap their fingers and think differently. They've got to learn to see.

So our well-considered auditor's recommendation is to start small and keep believing.

As a final thought, recall that we used A3 Thinking to develop the Active Auditing system. We defined our reason for action, mapped our current state, imagined a better target state, and experimented with solution approaches until we found something that worked. While I encourage you to try all the tools and techniques in this book, the odds are that you will need to conduct your own similar experiments.

I'd be surprised if across the profession our **Box 1 - Reasons for Action** are very different from one another. We all seem encumbered by far too much of the same Lean Waste.

However, to address that waste and make your audit process more efficient and effective, your solution approaches and rapid experiments probably should be different from ours. Make some changes and measure the outcome.

Remember that we always "reserve the right to get better."

GLOSSARY

>2 Week Section – A subsection of the Two-Week Panel that captures known tasks with deadlines greater than ten business days in the future.

8 Wastes – The common types of waste that Lean activities seek to eliminate or reduce. The 8 wastes are Defects, Overproduction, Waiting, Not utilizing human talent, Transportation, Inventory, Motion, and Excess processing. Often the acronym DOWNTIME is used as a mnemonic. Sometimes S-Safety is added as the 9th waste.

A3 – A tool used in Lean made up of 9 boxes, which intends to capture all components of a change or project on a single sheet of European-sized A3 paper. It contains spaces for the reason for action, the current state, target state, gap analysis, solutions approach, rapid experiments, completion plans, confirmed state, and insights.

A3 Thinking – Viewing change through the lens of the A3 tool and believing that all nine components matter. Also regards distilling problems and associated efforts to solve them with such clarity that they can fit and be expressed on a single sheet of paper.

Active Auditing – A management approach for internal audits that draws heavily on Lean & Agile principles and is built on the Three Pillars of Energetic Collaboration, Iterative Audit Execution, and Visual Management.

Agile – A software development methodology based on the Agile Manifesto from 2001 and built on a foundation of the 12 Agile Principles. Several variations of Agile development are in use today, including Scrum, Extreme Programming (XP), Crystal, and the Dynamic Systems Development Method (DSDM).

Control Objective (CO) – A short description of how the auditable business process should be working. COs are written "in the positive" and describe what should be happening. Fieldwork steps in audits are employed to determine whether the CO is being achieved.

Countermeasures – Actions to fix noted issues, installed in real-time as a result of making problems visible.

Daily Board – A subsection of the Two-Week Panel with columns for the next ten business days and on which are put task stickies. Communicates to the Single Combined Team the tasks that each member is working on relative to the audit.

Doghouse – A subsection of the Two-Week Panel into which are placed task stickies that are past due and impacting on-time completion of either the current Iteration or the entire audit. Task stickies in the Doghouse need immediate attention.

Energetic Collaboration – The habit of purposefully and constantly seeking to work closely together with audit clients.

Engagement Iteration Plan (EIP) – Similar to a Scrum "release schedule," the EIP assigns each Control Objective of an audit program (and the associated fieldwork necessary to evaluate it) to a time-boxed Iteration of the audit. It is expected that the initial EIP will change during the audit as more is known.

Experimentation – Intentionally promoting learning-by-trying and then measuring the outcome of changes to improve business processes, rather than assuming a chosen mitigation action plan will be better than what had been in place before.

Gemba – A Japanese and Lean term that means "going to where the work is done and opening your eyes." Reminds auditors that they must immerse themselves in the people and the work, and not merely rely on reports and work flows to understand how business processes work.

Gemba Walk – A deliberate activity to visit where the work is done and to make oneself open to learning. Depending on business process complexity, auditors may need to engage in a series of Gemba Walks to sufficiently increase their understanding. Auditors should only ask questions during Gemba Walks, and never telegraph potential issues or observations.

Governance Layer – The top-most level of an organization's governance structure. Usually made up of the organization's board and its executive team. When functioning appropriately, together this layer defines what success looks like organization-wide.

Harvey Bubble Table – A visual reporting tool or infographic approach that uses Harvey Balls or Harvey Bubbles to express the level of achievement of a Control Objective. For example, the auditors have evidence to declare a Control Objective almost entirely achieved, it may be appropriate to show it as a ¾ Harvey Bubble.

Hearts & Minds Panel – One of the five panels of an Active Auditing Visual Control Board (VCB), which makes visible the human aspects of an audit (e.g., anxieties, expectations, concerns, fears, hopes, and shared working agreements) so they can be managed.

IIA – Institute of Internal Auditors – the international professional association for members of the internal audit profession.

IPPF – International Professional Practices Framework, is the conceptual framework that organizes authoritative guidance promulgated by the IIA. It contains both mandatory guidance and recommended guidance. The mandatory guidance includes the Core Principles, Standards, and Code of Ethics.

Iteration – Similar to an Agile Sprint, a time-boxed chunk of an audit in which almost an entire cycle of a traditional auditing occurs from planning to workpaper review to issuance of observations. Iterations can be of varying lengths, though usually not longer than 4-5 weeks. Large audits may encompass several Iterations, while smaller audits may have only one.

Iterative Execution – The activity of apportioning fieldwork to time-boxed Iterations, coordinated by an Engagement Iteration Plan, to deliver audit results earlier and more frequently than would typically occur in a traditional "Waterfall" audit.

Just Do It Projects – Continuous improvement projects where the problem is simple, there appears to be a single, implementable solution, and the risk of failure appears low. Also called "quick wins."

Kaizen Event – Short duration improvement efforts with a targeted outcome; typically they are week-long events led by a facilitator, which are part of a larger schedule of continuous improvement work. The participants are predominantly members of the area in which the Kaizen Event is being conducted plus a few additional people from support areas, often playing roles as "fresh eyes." Sometimes customers and management participate. Rapid Improvement Events (RIEs), 5S Events, and Value Stream Mapping exercises are examples of Kaizen Events.

Lean – A collection of continuous improvement concepts, tools, and techniques with roots going as far back as Henry Ford, but owing much of their relevancy to the Toyota Production System (TPS) championed by Taiichi Ohno.

Lean Waste – One or more of the 8 Wastes that Lean activities seek to eliminate or reduce. The wastes are Defects, Overproduction, Waiting, Not utilizing human talent, Transportation, Inventory, Motion, and Excess processing. Often the acronym DOWNTIME is used as a mnemonic. Sometimes S-Safety is added as the 9th waste.

Management Layer – The middle layer of an organization's governance structure. This layer is responsible for ensuring the organization's objectives, defined by the Governance Layer, are achieved. Usually includes managers and directors.

Master Calendar – One of the five panels of an Active Auditing Visual Control Board (VCB), which captures and communicates availability of the Single Combined Team during the life of the audit and helps visualize important milestones.

Mitigating Action Plan – Management's plan for resolving issues coming out of an audit. Auditors may offer recommendations to management for the development of these plans, but the choice of action, including a decision by a member of the Governance Layer to accept the risk, is entirely owned by management. Under Active Auditing, mitigating action plans may be highly experimental in approach, ideally employing a metrics-based approach to determine whether the new business process is actually better than the old.

Muda – Activities that are non-value-added (NVA). Some Muda is unavoidable, at least for the moment. This is known as Type One Muda. Type Two Muda, which is usually represented by one of the 8 Wastes, can be diminished or eliminated by applying Lean techniques.

Mura – Unevenness or irregularity in workflow, which results in starting and stopping.

Muri – Overburdening people and processes by requiring them to run at a faster or longer pace than they should. Refers to "burning out" your system to achieve short term results in one period and often then idling that system or underutilizing it in the next period.

Mutual Purpose Gap – Represents the gap or difference between the auditor's and client's objectives in an audit. From the customer's point of view (e.g., the board) such a gap is unacceptable, yet internal audits have traditionally accepted significant mutual purpose gaps as unavoidable. As in any project, when all members of the team are not fully aligned, the project is likely to be more contentious, less efficient, and overall less successful.

NVA – Non-value-added work as seen from the customer's point of view.

Obeya – A dedicated location where Visual Management techniques can be used. Often thought of as a "war room," command center, or the "bridge" of a ship.

Panel – One of the Five Panels of the Active Auditing Visual Control Board (VCB. Some panels possess designated sub-sections or "Sections."

Performance Layer – The base layer of an organization's governance structure, which comprises line supervisors and employees who are executing instructions from the Management Layer.

Quick Win Projects – Continuous improvement projects where the problem is simple, there appears to be a single, implementable solution, and the risk of failure appears low. Also called "just do its."

Rapid Improvement Event – RIE for short, a form of Kaizen Event in which a team of employees is sequestered (often for a week) to improve a business process. The team is usually made up of employees doing the work, several "fresh eyes" participants, and sometimes customers. The goal of most RIEs is to produce a testable and measurable change at the end of the sequestration period.

Retrospective – A facilitated meeting, often 1.5 to 2 hours long, in which the members of an audit's Single Combined Team discuss how to make future audits better. Best done shortly after the reporting phase, when recollections are still fresh.

Scrum –An agile project management methodology/framework used for software development projects with the goal of delivering new software capability (e.g., usable and sellable code) roughly every 2-4 weeks.

Shared Agreements Panel – One of the five panels of an Active Auditing Visual Control Board (VCB), which captures and communicates Shared Ground Rules and Test Principles.

Single Combined Team – The unified project team tasked with on-time and on-scope delivery of an audit, which is made up of management and staff of both the auditors and the clients. Established to counter the traditional oppositional approach to audits and build mutual or shared purpose.

Sprint – A term used in Scrum software development to denote short, time-boxed periods (usually 2-4 weeks) where the scrum team works to complete a defined amount of work. In Active Auditing the analogous term is Iteration.

Standard Work – The best way we all know how to do a given process today. Standard work is necessary because if process participants do things differently, evaluating the effectiveness of change to the process becomes impossible. Standard work is usually written, but most importantly it is developed jointly and any changes to it are likewise made jointly with the involvement of the business process participants.

Story Point – Part of a common Scrum work and capacity estimating process. Story points represent a unit of measure for estimating the effort required to complete a part of a software development project. They encapsulate the amount of work, its complexity, and projected uncertainty around its completion.

Testing Principles – Often posted on the Shared Agreements Panel, these statements to clients describe how auditors are likely to evaluate the acceptability of fieldwork tests. By sharing these principles up front, ideally misunderstandings are avoided and feelings that the auditors are acting in an arbitrary way can be eliminated.

Two-Week Panel – One of the five panels of an Active Auditing Visual Control Board (VCB) which, through liberal use of colored sticky notes, communicates the work to be done over the next ten business days and helps members of the Single Combined Team visualize activities and progress. Includes three sub-sections – the Daily Board, >2 Week Section, and the Doghouse.

Variability – Well controlled business processes should produce expected outcomes continually. When they don't, this is regarded as variability. Business process variability is almost always unwelcome. Viewed in an IA context, fraud events are instances of unwanted variability. The business process should have prevented or detected fraud, and it didn't.

Value Stream – The notional collection of business processes that starts with raw material and completes with delivery of value to the customer. Used in Lean to connect chains of activities directly to customer value and make non-value-added work visible.

Value Stream Assessment – A strategic review of one or more value streams to identify opportunities for applying Lean and continuous improvement techniques.

Velocity – A common tool used in Scrum capacity planning, whereby a scrum team's capacity to complete tasks during a sprint is calculated in terms of story points. As sprints are planned, the story points of tasks assigned to that sprint are totaled to match the team's historic velocity. After each sprint, the team's velocity is reevaluated and may be adjusted up or down.

Visual Control Board – Tool used to make audit work visible to the Single Combined Team. Comprised of the five panels – Work Progress, Two-Week, Master Calendar, Shared Agreements, and Hearts & Minds.

Visual Management – A methodology and mindset based around making work, and obstacles to completion of that work, visible. Usually employs some form of Visual Control Board.

Waterfall – Widely used sequential project management methodology that relies on strong requirements gathering and design at the outset. Usually mid-project changes are not encouraged. Most construction projects employ a waterfall approach.

Work Progress Panel – One of the five panels of an Active Auditing Visual Control Board (VCB), which contains and communicates the work to be done based on the audit program (usually broken down by Control Objective) and the progress of the work towards completion.

INDEX

ABOUT THE AUTHOR

Prescott B. Coleman, CIA, CISA

For over 25 years, Prescott has provided consulting, auditing, and analytical services to all kinds of organizations.

After receiving a BA in Liberal Arts & Communications from Austin College, he began his career in Dallas as a small-business consultant. He and his wife moved to Colorado at the end of the 80's where he received an MBA from Colorado State University. From there he launched a marvelously diverse career, uniformly centered on organizational improvement.

Prescott has done work from every "column." In addition to his internal auditing career, he was a production floor manager, ran the treasury and investment operations for Colorado's third-largest city, and even helped colleges and universities in the U.S. and Canada develop strong, effective brands and marketing programs.

In auditing, he was part of the global audit leadership team for the 2nd largest property & casualty insurance company in the United Kingdom, and worked to build world-wide audit process consistency from their London headquarters. He built their U.S. IT Audit practice and created a team that provided high-value controls consulting for new projects and initiatives.

In 2009, he became the first Chief Internal Auditor for Denver Water, the most significant water utility in the western U.S., and over a 10 year period, helped it dramatically transform its operating and control environment.

It was at Denver Water, while immersed in the organization's uncompromising and highly successful "Lean journey" that Active Auditing was born.

Printed in Great Britain
by Amazon

19772885R00098